Robert K. O'Neill is Director of the John J. Burns Library at Boston College, Chestnut Hill, Massachusetts. He has held this position since 1987. He holds both the Ph.D in History and the MA in Library Science from the University of Chicago. Previously he was director of the Indiana Historical Society Library in Indianapolis and Head of Special Collections at Indiana State University, where he was also Associate Professor of Library Science in the College of Arts and Sciences.

His many publications include *English-Language Dictionaries, 1604-1900*, published by Greenwood Press, New York, in 1988. He has written numerous articles and reviews. He is currently editing a special issue of the *Journal of Library Administration* on Library security.

O'Neill is a past president of the Manuscript Society, 1992-1994 and the Eire Society of Boston, 1995-1997. He continues to serve as a member of the boards of both these organizations. He is also a member of the board of directors of Bookbuilders of Boston, and a member of the Grolier Club in New York and the Massachusetts Historical Society.

He is a Fellow of the Manuscripts Society, and received the Society's award of distinction. He was also honoured by the Irish and the American governments for his role in recovering stolen Irish artefacts in 1991.

He was a participant in the British Council-sponsored study tour of libraries in Northern Ireland in 1991.

O'Neill is married to the former Helen Ann Parke. The couple has six children. They live in Holliston, Massachusetts.

D1147504

LEABHARLANNA CHONTAE FHINE GALL
FINGAL COUNTY LIBRARIES

Items should be returned on or before the last date show
below. Items may be renewed by personal application,
writing or by telephone. To renew give the date due and t
number on the barcode label. Fines are charged on overd
items and will include postage incurred in recovery. Dama
to, or loss of items will be charged to the borrower.

Date Due	Date Due	Date Due

REFERENCE ONLY

First published 1997
by the Ulster Historical Foundation
12 College Square East, Belfast, BT1 6DD

ISBN 0-901905-79-8

Typeset by the Ulster Historical Foundation

Printed by ColourBooks Ltd

Cover and Design by Dunbar Design

This book has received support from the Cultural
Traditions Programme of the Community Relations
Council which aims to encourage acceptance and
understanding of cultural diversity.

CONTENTS

PREFACE

In 1991 I was invited to participate in a study tour of libraries and archives in Northern Ireland. The tour was sponsored by the British Council to introduce American librarians and archivists to information resources available in Northern Ireland and to promote cooperation among research institutions on both sides of the Atlantic. Following the ten-day tour we were asked to suggest ideas that might contribute to these ends. It seemed to me that the wealth of resources we examined would be of interest not only to librarians and research scholars but also to a much wider audience of Americans. For example, the 1990 American Census revealed that 44.3 million Americans claimed Irish ancestry. Many of these would be interested in tracing their ancestral roots in the north. Also, American businesses were rapidly expanding their involvement in Ireland, north and south, and access to pertinent information resources for this group would be essential.

I hesitated for some time to undertake this project. On the one hand it appeared presumptuous for a foreigner to prepare a guide to information resources in Northern Ireland, especially as there were so many distinguished professionals there who knew the library and archival landscape far better than I. On the other, an outsider enjoyed certain advantages. For starters, I would be able to approach the process from the eyes of a visitor, assuming nothing and taking nothing for granted. Visitors accustomed to the ways libraries and archives operate in their own countries are often not adequately prepared for the way things are done elsewhere. Differences can sometimes be significant, and protocol does matter. Many research institutions, for example, require advance notice, and much trouble, disappointment and expense can be avoided if researchers understand institutional requirements before they make their travel plans. Speaking of travel plans, a native would know intuitively not to plan a research trip to Northern Ireland during the July Twelfth Fortnight. Not so a visitor.

Another reason to go ahead with the project was that the kind of guide I proposed was simply not available. To be sure, there were some fine, standard reference sources for specific institutional categories, such as the *Directory of Libraries and Information Services in Ireland* and the *Directory of Irish Archives*. What I had in mind, though, was a handy, pocket-sized, visitor-friendly, comprehensive guide to research sources limited to Ulster that would include not only libraries and archives but also selected museums and ancestral heritage centres. Separate guides for Munster, Leinster and Connaght were to be considered later. The original guide was to have included only the six counties of historic Ulster located in Northern Ireland, but I was easily persuaded that the scope should be expanded to include all nine counties of Ulster. I also decided to include some museums and heritage centres that did not house research collections but whose focus might complement the interests of those visiting Ulster for research purposes. Since many researchers travel with family members, it seemed to make sense as well to offer non-researchers in the family interesting options. The option to visit some of the heritage centres and museums might also, I postulated, give family members a better understanding of and sympathy for the researcher's work. I tried this theory out with my own family, with mixed results, I hesitate to add.

What finally prompted me to go ahead with the project was the encouragement I received from friends in the library and archival world in the north of Ireland. Indeed, it would be difficult to exaggerate the tremendous cooperation I received from colleagues throughout Ulster. I therefore applied for and received research leave from Boston College that enabled me to spend the summer of 1995 in Ireland. Before departing I mailed out some 150 questionnaires. Response to questionnaires is often mixed at best; hence, I decided from the outset to visit personally as many institutions as possible. This not only helped me collect the data I needed but gave me first-hand experience of institutions to be included. Two more trips, one the following summer and one in February 1997, were required to complete my work.

The guide was originally intended primarily for academic and genealogical researchers, and the inclusion of branch or public libraries and some special libraries was to have been highly selective. But as I began to visit branch libraries, I often discovered hidden treasures, especially relating to local history. In addition, I began to appreciate that as tourism increased in Ulster, there would be a need for vacationers or family members of researchers simply to know if and what local libraries were available to them and what privileges they might enjoy. For example, it came as a pleasant surprise to me, as I am sure it would be to most American visitors, that access for foreigners to branch libraries, including borrowing privileges, was very generous in most cases. Furthermore, these branch libraries are often the best source for information on what's happening locally.

I have tried to make this guide to libraries as comprehensive as possible, but certain libraries were omitted...some at their own request, some because they are not open to visitors, some so specialized they would be of very limited interest to visitors, and others that I simply overlooked. I became aware too late of a few libraries that should have been included in the first edition of this guide. I will correct this oversight in the next edition.

ACKNOWLEDGEMENTS

This guide would not have been possible without the help of a good many people. Acknowledgements must start with Marie Daley of the New England Genealogical Society who nominated me for the study tour, and to Peter Lyner and Carmel McGill of the British Council who acted favourably on Marie's nomination. Welsey McCann, Librarian of Stranmillis College in Belfast and director of the tour, was exceedingly generous in his encouragement and in his assistance from the moment I first proposed the idea of the guide to him to his reading of a draft of the manuscript. Stranmillis College served as my home and base of operations for two months in the summer of 1995. The entire staff, especially the Halls staff, made me and my children feel very welcome. I am especially indebted to Maurice and Mary Blease, who made the housing arrangements and who extended their assistance and every courtesy possible throughout my stay. Indeed, the entire Blease family, including children Johnnie, Sarah and Emma; Maurice's father, Lord William Blease, and brother, Victor Blease, went out of their way to make us feel at home. Space does not permit me to list all of the good people at Stranmillis who, like the Bleases, made our stay such a warm and memorable one, but I would like to thank in particular Norman Halliday, Bursar of the College: Katherine Anderson, Halls Supervisor; Dr Eamon Phoenix, history professor, and Dr J.R.B. McMinn, Principal of the College, for their many courtesies and kindnesses. Jack and Jean Gamble of Emerald Isle Books, Belfast, not only generously extended their hospitality on numerous occasions but read the entire manuscript and offered invaluable suggestions and encouragement. My son Dan still speaks in awe about the "twelve-course tea" they served us on one of the many happy visits to their beautiful home. I am extremely grateful also to the many librarians, archivists and curators throughout Ulster who not only took the time to complete my questionnaire and to share their time and expertise, but also because they invariably offered me tea. I am also grateful to both the Public Record Office of Northern Ireland, Belfast and the National Archives, Dublin for their permission to list, as an appendix to this book, the references to their tithe and valuation holdings for the parishes of Ulster.

To the good people at the Ulster Historical Foundation, I want to express special thanks. Shane McAteer, Secretary of the Ulster Historical Foundation, was enthusiastic and supportive from the outset. Talented designer Wendy Dunbar made several very important contributions to the format of the final work. George Woodman, consultant to the Foundation, read the entire manuscript and made several helpful suggestions to improve the work. No words of appreciation, however, can adequately express the debt I owe and the gratitude I feel towards Dr. Brian Trainor, former Director of the Public Record Office of Northern Ireland and current Research Director of the Ulster Historical Foundation. Dr Trainor gave unstintingly of his time and hospitality in assisting me to complete this work. His knowledge, expertise and contacts were always at my disposal. Dr. Trainor strongly encouraged me to expand the guide to include Counties Cavan, Monaghan and Donegal, and made it possible for me to do so by driving me to various sites in these counties. I would be especially remiss if I did not thank Brian's wife, Pilar, who opened her home to me and prepared such wonderful meals. One of the great joys of undertaking this work has been the many friendships I developed, and it would be virtually impossible to repay all the kindness I received. The hospitality of the people in the nine counties of Ulster is worth the trip alone, and I regret that space does not permit me to acknowledge individually all those who were so helpful to me.

Boston College not only provided me leave time to visit libraries and archives throughout Ulster but also provided invaluable support services. Dorothy McLaughlin, my administrative assistant, was especially helpful in assisting me with the vast amount of correspondence connected with this project. University Librarians Mary Cronin and Jerome Yavarkovsky strongly supported this effort. The Irish American Partnership and the American Ireland Fund provided grants that helped considerably to make possible the on site visits necessary to complete this project in a timely fashion. Special thanks to Joseph F. Leary, Jr., President and Chief Executive Officer of the Partnership, and to Kingsley Aikins, Executive Director of the AIF, for their special support and encouragement. Thanks also to Thomas P. O'Neill, III, a Trustee of AIF, for taking a personal interest in this guide. A very special thank you to my wife Helen and our children Kathleen, Kevin, Kerry, Daniel, MaryAnn and Timothy. Kathleen, Kerry and Dan were my companions in Belfast in the summer of 1995, and they not only made the long absence from home more tolerable but helped to provide a critical perspective to my work. Finally, I dedicate this book to the memory of my mother, Mary Veronica Leahy O'Neill, the daughter of Hannah Duffin Leahy of Moneyglass, County Antrim, and Michael Leahy of Tullamore, County Kerry. From early on my mother instilled in me tremendous love, respect and pride in my Irish heritage. This is my small way of saying thank you.

HELPFUL HINTS FOR VISITORS

SCHEDULING YOUR TRIP!

Please consult carefully the times listed for each of the institutions you might want to visit. All times are subject to change, and it is advisable to check in advance with the institution. If you can travel in September or May, this might be the best time to visit Ireland. The weather is generally very good, but, more important, most of the places you will want to visit will be open. While the most popular, and, for many, the most convenient time to travel is the summer, keep in mind that some institutions close for part of the summer. Most important, in Northern Ireland avoid the Twelfth of July week if you can. Virtually all libraries and archives are closed the 12th and 13th of July, many for the entire Twelfth week, and some for the Twelfth fortnight.

GETTING THERE!

Aer Lingus introduced once-a-week direct flights to Belfast via Shannon from the United States in the summer of 1995. More frequent departures may be added, however, if demand warrants. Consult with your travel agent. Direct flights to Dublin are now available on Aer Lingus from Chicago, Boston and New York, and on Delta from Atlanta. Aer Lingus does not operate out of Canada. World Airlines operates a Charter service to Shannon/Dublin from May through September. Other charter services may also be available to Ireland. If you are going north from Dublin, the rail service from Connolly Station is convenient, fast and reasonably priced. A new, high-speed service is being introduced on the Dublin-Belfast run. If you are flying into Belfast from London's Heathrow Airport, British Airways and British Midlands offer several flights daily. *Caveat viator*! If you are flying out of Heathrow, be sure to allow extra time for security checks.

TO RENT A CAR OR NOT!

If your plans call for spending all or most of your time in Belfast, a car rental, i.e., car hire, is not necessary. All of the major information resource centres in Belfast are easily accessible by public transportation. Belfast has good bus and rail services, and the taxi service is modestly priced, even by American standards. Taxi services, however, may provide you with your first experience with the reality of a divided community. Taxis are often identified along Nationalist or Unionist lines, and one will not go into the other's community, e.g. the Falls (Nationalist), Shankill (Unionist). You need not be alarmed, however. The driver will simply ask you your destination, and if he (I have never seen a female taxi driver in Belfast, though there may be some) will not go there, he will direct you to a taxi that will. People on both sides of the divide are pleased to welcome visitors from abroad, and they will go out of their way to accommodate you. Most of the major libraries and archives are located in mixed areas, so this should not be a problem in any case.

If you need to venture beyond Belfast or Derry, a car rental is advised, unless you are prepared to hire a car and driver. You are already aware no doubt that cars are driven on the left-hand side of the road in all of Ireland, but what you may not be aware of is how difficult it is to find a rental with automatic transmission. These are generally available only on the higher-priced models, and often have to be booked far in advance. If you haven't driven a stick shift in a while, you may want to practice a bit before you head off to Ireland. If you heed no other piece of advice offered in this guide, heed this: **Enter roundabouts (rotaries) on the left.**

TWO PEOPLES DIVIDED BY A COMMON LANGUAGE!

Attributed to Shaw. American visitors may find certain unfamiliar spellings and phraseologies throughout this guide. But when in Rome...! Since this guide is being published in Belfast, English-English orthography and usage apply. Hence, jail is gaol, artifact is artefact, center is centre, catalog is catalogue; parking lot is car park, etc. Not all words that are pronounced the same but spelled differently mean the same, however. It is legal and perfectly fine to enjoy "craic" throughout Ulster, but if you go looking for "crack", as in "crack-cocaine", the consequences could be severe. "Craic" is the Irish expression for a good time, and it is totally unrelated to "crack". Some terms may also be confusing to American tourists not familiar with the political history of the Troubles. Many Americans, for example, assume Unionists refer to those people who favour a United Ireland. Quite the contrary. Unionists support the Act of Union of 1800 which abolished the Irish Parliament and brought Ireland into the United Kingdom. Unionists wish to remain part of Great Britain; Nationalists support a United Ireland entirely independent of Great Britain.

AHOGHILL BRANCH LIBRARY
Brook Street
AHOGHILL, BT42 1LD

TELEPHONE: 01266–871768

HOURS:
TUE: 2:00 pm–5:00 pm, 6:00 pm–8:00 pm;
TH: 10:30 am–1:00 pm, 2:00 pm–5:30 pm;
FRI: 2:00 pm–5:00 pm, 6:00 pm–8:00 pm;
SAT: 10:30 am–1:00 pm, 2:00 pm–5:00 pm

ACCESS:
Visitors welcome, but identification required. Borrowing
privileges for visitors may be restricted. Consult with
Librarian.

CONTACT PERSON: Mrs. L. McFadden, Senior Library
Assistant in charge

SEE ALSO: NORTH EASTERN EDUCATION AND LIBRARY
BOARD, Ballymena

ANTRIM BRANCH LIBRARY
41 Church Street
ANTRIM, BT41 4BE

TELEPHONE: 01849–461942

HOURS:
MON, WED, FRI: 10:00 am–1:00 pm, 2:00 pm–5:30 pm;
TUE, TH: 10:30 am–1:00 pm, 2:00 pm–5:00 pm, 5:30 pm
–8:00 pm;
SAT: 10:00 am–1:00 pm, 2:00 pm–5:00 pm

ACCESS:
Visitors welcome, but identification required. Borrowing
privileges for visitors may be restricted. Consult with
Librarian.

CONTACT PERSON: Mrs. C. Carey, Senior Library
Assistant in charge

SEE ALSO: NORTH EASTERN EDUCATION AND LIBRARY BOARD,
Ballymena

ARMAGH CITY:

(NOTE: All the following listings are located in or near the City Centre, within easy walking distance of one another, with two exceptions, the Southern Education and Library Board and its special Irish Studies Library and The Navan Centre.)

ARMAGH ANCESTRY
42 English Street
ARMAGH, BT61 7BA

TELEPHONE: 01861–521802; FAX: 01861–510033

HOURS:
MON–SAT: 9:00 am–5:00 pm

ACCESS:
Private and publicly-funded genealogical service centre open to the public. For schedule of fees, contact the Supervisor.

CONTACT PERSON: Grace Greer, Supervisor

DESCRIPTION:
Armagh Ancestry, established in 1992, is one of seven centres in the nine counties of Ulster that participate in the Irish Genealogical Project (IGP), an effort to create a comprehensive genealogical database for all Ireland from a wide variety of sources, including church and state records, vital records, tithe applotment books, Griffith's valuation, the 1901 census, and gravestone inscriptions. Armagh Ancestry offers a genealogical research service for County Armagh. Computerization of genealogical records for County Armagh has been underway since 1985. Completed records include all the County Armagh Catholic registers up to 1900; Civil Births 1864–1922 and Marriages 1845-1922; some Protestant registers up to 1900. Currently, the Centre is inputting Civil Deaths 1864–1922 and pre-1900 Church registers of all denominations.

SERVICES:
The centre offers a small genealogical library for consultation, with special emphasis on Armagh. The centre also sells locally produced crafts, family crests, ancestral tree charts, maps, and material of a genealogical interest. In addition to library services, the centre offers professional genealogical research services, and even a genealogical tour planned around the visitor's family history. Fees vary depending on service

and time involved. Currently, these range from £10 to £150. Brochures are available. Public car parks nearby.

SEE ALSO:
ULSTER HISTORICAL FOUNDATION, Belfast; CAVAN GENEALOGICAL RESEARCH CENTRE, Cavan; THE GENEALOGY CENTRE, Derry; HERITAGE WORLD, Dungannon; MONAGHAN ANCESTRY, Monaghan; and DONEGAL ANCESTRY, Ramelton. Also: GENERAL REGISTER OFFICE, Belfast; and PUBLIC RECORD OFFICE OF NORTHERN IRELAND, Belfast.

ARMAGH BRANCH LIBRARY
Market Street
ARMAGH, BT61 7BU

TELEPHONE: 01861-524072

HOURS:
MON, FRI: 9:30 am–6:00 pm;
TUE, TH: 9:30 am–8:00 pm;
WED, SAT: 9:30 am–5:00 pm

ACCESS:
Visitors welcome, identification required. Borrowing privileges for visitors may be restricted. Consult with Librarian. Handicapped accessible.

CONTACT PERSON: Miss Cathy Pomeroy, Librarian

DESCRIPTION:
General collection, including audio-visual materials, with good reference collection and current newspaper and periodical collection.

SERVICES:
Photocopying; local announcements; audio and videotape rentals.

SEE ALSO: SOUTHERN EDUCATION AND LIBRARY BOARD, Armagh

ARMAGH COUNTY MUSEUM
The Mall East
ARMAGH, BT61 9BE

TELEPHONE: 01861–523070; FAX: 01861–522631

HOURS:
MON–FRI: 10:00 am–5:00 pm;
SAT: 10:00 am–1:00 pm, 2:00 pm–5:00 pm

ACCESS:
Publicly–funded museum whose library and exhibits are
open to public free of charge; library stacks closed.
Advance notification by letter (at least 2 weeks)
required for permission to use research collections. Card
catalogue. Will be handicapped accessible from 1998.

CONTACT PERSON: Catherine McCullough, Curator

DESCRIPTION:
Armagh County Museum is a branch of the Ulster
Museum, Belfast. A community museum focusing on the
County of Armagh, it houses one of the finest county
collections in Ireland. Museum holdings include art
works, archaeological objects, local and natural history
specimens, textile, railway and military artefact
collections. Paintings of note include John Luke's "The
Old Callan Bridge," and pastels by George Russell. The
Museum's Library houses approximately 10,000
volumes and 48 linear feet of manuscripts
plus a small collection of photographs. The Library is
especially strong in local history, with important
collections of maps and prints. Subject areas include
archaeology, history, folk and rural life, fine arts and
crafts, natural history, military and costume relating to
the County of Armagh. The Museum is housed in a
distinctive, classical revival building, which first opened
in 1834 as a school.

SPECIAL COLLECTIONS:
The TGF Paterson manuscript collection, including
working papers with notes on local families and
buildings: *Armaghiana* Vols. 1–24, including Paterson's
typed notes with indexes; journals (7 vols.) of William
Blacker (1777–1855), including local notes and jottings
with an account of the Battle of the Diamond (1795);
manuscripts and illustrated poems of George Russell
(AE), (1867–1935).

SERVICES:
Photocopying; free public parking outside Museum.

RESTRICTIONS:
No pens, only pencils. Battery-operated PCs allowed
with permission.

PUBLICATIONS:
*Harvest Home, The Last Sheaf: A Selection of the
Writings of T. G. F. Paterson Relating to County Armagh*
(Armagh, 1975).

SEE ALSO:
CAVAN COUNTY MUSEUM, Ballyjamesduff; NORTH DOWN
HERITAGE CENTRE, Bangor; ULSTER MUSEUM, Belfast;
TOWER MUSEUM, Derry; DOWN COUNTY MUSEUM;
Downpatrick; ENNISKILLEN CASTLE, Enniskillen; ULSTER
FOLK AND TRANSPORT MUSEUM, Cultra; DONEGAL COUNTY
MUSEUM, Letterkenny; IRISH LINEN CENTRE AND LISBURN
MUSEUM, Lisburn; MONAGHAN COUNTY MUSEUM,
Monaghan; and ULSTER-AMERICAN FOLK PARK, Omagh.

ARMAGH DIOCESAN ARCHIVES
Ara Coeli
ARMAGH, BT61 7QY

TELEPHONE: 01861–522045; FAX: 01861–526182

HOURS:
By appointment

ACCESS:
Private (Roman Catholic) archives open to the public by
appointment only. Advance notice and letter of reference
required. Copying may be restricted. The papers from
Archbishop O'Reilly (1793) to Cardinal D'Alton (d.
1963) have been catalogued. Papers up to c. 1900 have
been calendered in full in volumes of typescript with
indexes. A new archive facility is planned.

CONTACT PERSON: Rev. Diocesan Secretary

DESCRIPTION:
The Armagh Archives houses the papers of the
archbishops of Armagh from the late 1700s to the
present. The Archives is expected to be housed
eventually in the new Cardinal Ó Fiaich Library,
scheduled to open on March 17, 1998.

SPECIAL COLLECTIONS:
Leather-bound volume of 257 original letters from
Archbishop O'Reilly to his vicar-general, Dr. Conwell,
between 1793 and 1813; the D'Alton, Conway and
Fiaich archives are of special interest.

SERVICES:
Photocopying; ample free parking.

SEE ALSO:
ARMAGH RECORDS CENTRE, Armagh; and THE CARDINAL
TOMÁS Ó FIAICH MEMORIAL LIBRARY & ARCHIVE, Armagh.

A

ARMAGH OBSERVATORY
College Hill
ARMAGH, BT61 9DG

TELEPHONE: 01861–522928; FAX: 01861–527174;
E-MAIL: jmf@star.arm.ac.uk;
WEB SITE: http://star.arm.ac.uk

HOURS:
MON–FRI: 9:00 am–5:00 pm

ACCESS:
Publicly-funded, non-circulating library and archives
open to researchers by appointment; advance notice by
letter to librarian required; stacks open except for
special collections. The entire collection is catalogued
on cards; a printed catalogue for part of the collection is
also available.

CONTACT PERSON: John McFarland, Librarian

DESCRIPTION:
The Observatory was founded in 1790 by Archbishop
Richard Robinson, Church of Ireland Primate, who also
founded the Armagh Public Library. The Observatory
continues to function as an important player in
astronomical research, and its library and archives,
housed in the Observatory's original Georgian mansion,
seek to maintain a centralized Northern Ireland
astronomical collection. In addition to astronomy, the
library has strong holdings in mathematics, physics and
astrophysics. It currently holds approximately 1,600
books, 5,000 photographs, 200 linear feet of
manuscripts, and a very strong collection of some 15,000
journal volumes. The archives contain documents
relating to the administration of the Observatory,
observations, meteorological records, personal papers
and astronomical drawings. The Observatory also houses
an important collection of historical instruments;
manuscripts by J.L.E. Dreyer.

SPECIAL COLLECTIONS:
T. R. Robinson (1792-1882) Collection of Rare and
Antiquarian Books (200 vols.); Papers of J. A. Hamilton;
Papers of T. R. Robinson.

SERVICES:
Photocopying; limited free parking; brochure.

PUBLICATIONS:
Armagh Observatory Preprint Series; Moore, Patrick.
Armagh Observatory: A History, 1790-1967. Armagh,
1967.

BIBLIOGRAPHY:
Bennett, J. A. *Church, State and Astronomy in Ireland:
200 Years of Armagh Observatory* (Armagh, 1990).
Butler, John., and Michael Hoskin. "The Archives of
Armagh Observatory." *Journal of the History of
Astronomy* 18 (1987): 295-307.; McFarland, John. "The
Historical Instruments of Armagh Observatory," *Vistas
in Astronomy*. 33 (1990): 149-210.; "The Rare and
Antiquarian Book Collection of the Armagh
Observatory." *The Irish Astronomical Journal*. 18
(1987): 102-115.

ARMAGH PUBLIC LIBRARY
Abbey Street
ARMAGH, BT61 7DY

TELEPHONE: 01861–523142; FAX: 01861–524177

HOURS:
MON–FRI: 10:00 am–1:00 pm, 2:00 pm–4:00 pm;
or, by appointment

ACCESS:
Private, non-circulating library, open to public.
Currently, admission is free but donations appreciated.
A fee schedule for reader services and tours has recently
been introduced and is available upon request. There is
a card catalogue for the book collection and a printed
catalogue for the manuscript collection. Linked by
computer with the Library and Education Boards closed
network operated by Belfast City Council Computer
Services. Prefer advance notice for specific research
requests. Not handicapped accessible.

CONTACT PERSON: William Robert H. Carson, Librarian

DESCRIPTION:
The Armagh Public Library, also known as the Robinson
Library, was founded in 1771 by Archbishop Richard
Robinson, Church of Ireland Primate, who also founded
the Armagh Observatory. The Library houses some
20,000 volumes, including the Archbishop's personal
collection of early books on history, canon and civil law,
heraldry, literature, medicine, philosophy, religion,

A

theology and travel. The Robinson Collection is fully integrated into the library's collection, which has been enhanced over the past two centuries chiefly by other clerical collections. In recent times the Library has concentrated on ecclesiastical history, St. Patrick and Jonathan Swift. Book highlights include incunabula, Colgan's *Acta Sanctorum Hiberniae* (1645), a Breeches Bible and a first edition of *Gulliver's Travels,* with marginal emendations in Swift's own hand. There is also a fine map collection. The manuscript collection includes medieval and early modern European items, many of an Irish interest, especially concerning lands and tithes records.

SPECIAL COLLECTIONS:
Archbishop's Robinson's Collection of Engravings, known as the "Rokeby Collection;" Archbishop Marcus Gervais Beresford's Collection of Irish artefacts.

SERVICES:
Photocopying; ample free parking; collection browsing.

RESTRICTIONS:
No pens; consult librarian for use of typewriters, computers and cameras; no bags allowed.

BIBLIOGRAPHY:
Dean, James. *Catalogue of Manuscripts in the Public Library of Armagh 1928*. Dundalk: The Governors and Guardians, 1928. McKelvie, Colin. "Early English Books in Armagh Public Library: A Short-title Catalogue of Book Printed before 1641." *Irish Booklore* 3: 91-103.

ARMAGH RECORDS CENTRE
Ara Coeli
ARMAGH, BT61 7QY

TELEPHONE: 01861-522981

HOURS:
By appointment

ACCESS:
Private centre sponsored by the Catholic Archdiocese of Armagh. Services are available to the public. Requests by mail preferred. Computerized database not accessible to public at this time. Fees may apply. Entrance to the Centre is near St. Patrick's Grammar School.

CONTACT PERSON: Caroline Hicks, Director

A

DESCRIPTION:
The Armagh Records Centre is computerizing pre-1900 Catholic parish registers of the Archdiocese of Armagh. These registers contain baptismal, marriage and death records of residents within each parish boundary. NOTE: Few records of death were kept. The Archdiocese covers 60 Catholic parishes spread over three counties: most of Armagh, a large part of Tyrone and all of Louth. The Centre works in cooperation with ARMAGH ANCESTRY, and inquiries may be referred there.

SERVICES:
The Records Centre is not a genealogical service, but it is willing to carry out certain services using its database. A brochure listing the parishes and the years for which records are available has been published.

SEE ALSO: ARMAGH ANCESTRY, Armagh

THE CARDINAL TOMÁS Ó FIAICH MEMORIAL LIBRARY & ARCHIVE
Ara Coeli
ARMAGH, BT61 7QY

TELEPHONE: 01861–522905

HOURS:
Not applicable. Collection closed to the public at present; scheduled to open in 1998.

ACCESS:
The Library is temporarily housed in the Archdiocesan Records Centre facility pending construction of a dedicated library and archive. Construction was scheduled to begin in early 1997. A private, non-circulating library, the collection is catalogued in machine readable form on an in-house, closed system. No access available at this time.

CONTACT PERSON: Brother Dermot McDermott, Curator

DESCRIPTION:
The Library houses the books and papers of Cardinal Tomás Ó Fiaich (1923-1990), Archbishop of Armagh and Catholic Primate of All Ireland. The Library contains approximately 10,000 volumes and nearly 600 periodical titles arranged by subject. Of special interest are: Early and Modern Irish History, Hagiography, Irish Saints, especially St. Patrick and St. Oliver Plunkett, County

Histories, Irish Language, Literature, Music, Art and
Genealogy. There is also a good collection of maps and
atlases. The Cardinal's library will be enhanced by other
diocesan collections and purchases. Special emphasis
will be on Irish history, especially ecclesiastical history,
Irish culture, especially Irish language and Irish games,
and Irish-European and Irish-American links.

SERVICES:
Photocopying, ample free parking.

IRISH STUDIES LIBRARY
(LOCAL HISTORY LIBRARY)
SOUTHERN EDUCATION AND LIBRARY BOARD
HEADQUARTERS
1 Markethill Road
ARMAGH, BT60 1NR
TELEPHONE: 01861–525353; FAX: 01861–526879

HOURS:
MON, TH. AND FRI: 9:30 am–5:00 pm;
TUE–WED: 9:30 am–7:15 pm

ACCESS:
Visitors welcome. Sign in at HQ reception desk. Entire
collection of books and manuscripts catalogued in
machine readable form. Most of the collection is in the
Reading Room, but about a quarter of the books and all
of the journals are in the closed stacks. Linked to the
emigration database of the Ulster-American Folk Park.
Handicapped accessible. Located on the outskirts of
Armagh City, on the road to Markethill and Newry.
PLEASE NOTE. Library may be relocated to the new
Queen's Centre in Armagh City.

CONTACT PERSON: Miss M. McVeigh, Irish Studies
Librarian

DESCRIPTION:
The library was established in 1975 as part of the
Southern Education and Library Board. It collects in all
areas of Irish and local studies, with special emphasis on
the border areas, past and present. It houses some
20,000 volumes, 350 journal titles, 3,000 maps, 3,800
microforms, 50 newspapers, 1,500 pamphlets and 2,500
photographs. It also has a small collection of manuscript
records.

SPECIAL COLLECTIONS:
Pamphlet collection on late 18th and early 19th century
Irish political and economic history; Francis Crossle
Manuscript Collection on the Newry area, including
some 200 notebooks compiled by Dr. Crossle containing
histories of families in the Newry area.

SERVICES:
Photocopying; brochure; free parking.

PUBLICATIONS:
"Irish Railway Literature: A Select List of Publications"

SEE ALSO: SOUTHERN EDUCATION AND LIBRARY BOARD,
Armagh

THE NAVAN CENTRE
81 Killea Road
ARMAGH, BT16 4LD

TELEPHONE: 01861–525550; FAX: 01861–522323

HOURS:
APRIL, JUNE, AND SEPTEMBER:
MON.– SAT: 10:00 am–6:00 pm,
SUN: 11:00 am–6:00 pm;
JULY–AUGUST:
MON–SAT: 10:00 am–7:00 pm,
SUN: 11:00 am–7:00 pm;
OCTOBER–MARCH:
MON–FRI: 10:00 am–5:00 pm,
SAT: 11:00 am–5:00 pm;
SUN: 12:00 am–5:00 pm;
CLOSED Christmas week

ACCESS:
Open to the general public. Admission charged. Current
admission fees: Adults = £3.95; Children = £2.25.
Special family, group, senior, and student rates
available.

CONTACT PERSON: Paddy Dillon, Administration Officer

DESCRIPTION:
Located two miles west of Armagh City Centre, The
Navan Centre interprets the great mound of Navan Fort,
or Emain Macha, the ancient seat of the Kings of Ulster
dating back to 94 BC and the earliest capital of Ulster. A
system of earthworks, settlement sites and sacred places,
Navan Fort is considered Northern Ireland's most

important ancient monument. The visitor centre offers exhibits and shows interpreting some 7,500 years of activity in this area through archaeological finds and ancient Celtic rituals, legends and beliefs.

SERVICES:
Multi-language translations of exhibition/show; restaurant; souvenir gift shop; parking.

SEE ALSO: SAINT PATRICK'S TRIAN, Armagh

SAINT PATRICK'S TRIAN
40 English Street
ARMAGH, BT61 7DY

TELEPHONE: 01861–521801; FAX: 01861–528329

HOURS:
APRIL–SEPTEMBER:
MON–SAT: 10:00 am–7:00 pm,
SUN: 1:00 pm–7:00 pm;
OCTOBER–MARCH:
MON–SAT: 10:00 am–5:00 pm,
SUN: 2:00 pm–5:00 pm

ACCESS:
Open to the general public. Admission charged. Current admission charges: Adults = £3.25; Children (ages 4-15) = £1.60; Children under 4 = free; Seniors = £2.40. Special family and group rates available. Handicapped accessible.

CONTACT PERSON: Director, Saint Patrick's Trian

DESCRIPTION:
Located in the centre of Armagh City, the Trian (a name derived from the ancient division of Armagh City into distinct quarters) is a tourist complex that illustrates the history of Armagh City from pre-historic times to the present. Featured displays include "The Land of Lilliput," a child-centred fantasy experience based on Swift's *Gulliver's Travels*. Special events include: art exhibitions, permanent exhibition on St. Patrick, literary, educational and historical programmes (of religious significance), classical and traditional music and themed children's events.

SERVICES:
Tourist information; restaurant; genealogical research centre; public car parks.

SEE ALSO: THE NAVAN CENTRE, Armagh

SOUTHERN EDUCATION AND LIBRARY BOARD
LIBRARY HEADQUARTERS
1 Market Hill Road
ARMAGH, BT60 1NR

TELEPHONE: 01861–525353; FAX: 01861–526879

HOURS:
MON-FRI: 8:30 am–5:30 pm;
Hours for special collections vary. See below.

ACCESS:
By appointment. Located on the outskirts of Armagh City, on the road to Markethill and Newry.

CONTACT PERSON: Andrew Morrow, Chief Librarian

DESCRIPTION:
The SELB was established in 1973 as the administrative headquarters for 3 divisional libraries (CRAIGAVON, DUNGANNON and NEWRY) and 23 branch libraries (ARMAGH, BANBRIDGE, BESSBROOK, BROWNLOW, COALISLAND, COOKSTOWN, CROSSMAGLEN, DROMORE, DUNGANNON, FIVEMILETOWN, GILFORD, KEADY, KILKEEL, LURGAN, MONEYMORE, MOY, NEWRY, PORTADOWN, RATHFRILAND, RICHHILL, TANDRAGEE, WARINGSTOWN and WARRENPOINT.) Each of these libraries, except Warrenpoint, may be found in this Guide under its own heading by city or town. In addition to public libraries, SELB operates school, special service and mobile libraries. At its headquarters, SELB operates an Irish Studies Library and a Hospitals & Associated Services Section. The former is treated separately above. The combined holdings of the branch, divisional and special libraries is approximately 1.5 million volumes.

SPECIAL COLLECTIONS:
SEE IRISH STUDIES LIBRARY, Armagh

ARVA BRANCH LIBRARY
SEE CAVAN COUNTY COUNCIL BRANCH LIBRARIES, Cavan

B

BAILIEBOROUGH BRANCH LIBRARY
Market House
BAILIEBOROUGH, COUNTY CAVAN

TELEPHONE: 049–65779

HOURS:
MON: 10:30 am–2:00 pm, 3:00 pm–6:00 pm;
TUE, TH: 10:30 am–1:00 pm, 2:00 pm–5:15 pm;
FRI: 10:30 am–1:00 pm, 2:00 pm–5:15 pm, 6:00 pm–
8:00 pm;
SAT: 2:30 pm–5:15 pm.

ACCESS:
Visitors welcome. Borrowing privileges restricted.
Consult with Librarian. Handicapped accessible. Books
arranged by Dewey. Catalogue available at Cavan only.

CONTACT PERSON: Mr. Bernard Kettle, Branch Librarian;
Mrs. Josephine Brady, County Librarian

DESCRIPTION:
Former Market House converted to library in 1992.
Houses about 15,000 volumes. Good local history
collection, including Griffith's Valuation for most of
Cavan.

SERVICES:
Photocopier; local flyers and brochures.

SEE ALSO: CAVAN COUNTY COUNCIL BRANCH LIBRARIES,
Cavan

BALLEE BRANCH LIBRARY
2 Neighbourhood Centre
BALLEE, BALLYMENA, BT42 2SX

TELEPHONE: 01266–45761

HOURS:
TUE: 10:30 am–1:00 pm, 2:00 pm–5:30 pm;
WED: 2:00 pm–5:30 pm;
FRI: 2:00 pm–5:30 pm, 6:00 pm–8:00 pm;
SAT: 10:00 am–1:00 pm, 2:00 pm–5:00 pm

ACCESS:
Visitors welcome, but identification required. Borrowing

privileges for visitors may be restricted. Consult with Librarian.

CONTACT PERSON: Mrs. R. Dickey, Senior Library Assistant in charge

SEE ALSO: NORTH EASTERN EDUCATION AND LIBRARY BOARD, Ballymena

BALLINAGH BRANCH LIBRARY
SEE CAVAN COUNTY COUNCIL BRANCH LIBRARIES, Cavan

BALLYBAY BRANCH LIBRARY
Main Street
BALLYBAY, COUNTY MONAGHAN
TELEPHONE: 042–41256

HOURS:
MON, FRI: 7:00 pm–9:00 pm;
TUE, WED: 3:00 pm–6:00 pm

ACCESS:
Visitors welcome, but identification required. Borrowing privileges are available for visitors but may be limited. Consult with Librarian.

CONTACT PERSON: Senior Library Assistant

SEE ALSO: MONAGHAN COUNTY LIBRARY, Clones

BALLYBOFEY BRANCH LIBRARY
SEE DONEGAL COUNTY LIBRARY ADMINISTRATIVE CENTRE, Letterkenny

BALLYCASTLE BRANCH LIBRARY
5 Leyland Road
BALLYCASTLE, BT54 6DT

TELEPHONE: 012657–62566

HOURS:
MON, FRI: 10:30 am–1:00 pm, 2:00 pm–5:30 pm;
TUE, TH: 10:30 am–1:00 pm, 2:00 pm–5:30 pm, 6:00 pm –8:00 pm;
SAT: 10:30 am–1:00 pm, 2:00 pm–5:00 pm

ACCESS:
Visitors welcome, but identification required. Borrowing
privileges for visitors may be restricted. Consult with
Librarian. Handicapped accessible.

CONTACT PERSON: Miss Joan Coyles, Senior Library
Assistant in charge

DESCRIPTION:
Branch Library of the NEELB, with a collection of about
16,000 volumes plus small holdings of microforms and
recordings, plus 3 newspapers.

SERVICES:
Microfiche reader; local brochures available; limited
parking.

SEE ALSO: NORTH EASTERN EDUCATION AND LIBRARY
BOARD, Ballymena

BALLYCLARE BRANCH LIBRARY
The Market House, School Street
BALLYCLARE BT39 9BE

TELEPHONE: 019603–52269

HOURS:
TUE, FRI: 10:00 am–8:00 pm;
WED: 10:00 am–5:30 pm;
SAT: 10 am–5:00 pm

ACCESS:
Visitors welcome, but identification required. Borrowing
privileges for visitors may be restricted. Consult with
Librarian. Handicapped accessible.

CONTACT PERSON: Mrs. C. Kane, Principal Library
Assistant in charge

DESCRIPTION:
Branch Library of NEELB with a collection of some
32,000 volumes, plus modest holdings of journals,
microforms, newspapers and recordings. Local studies
collection includes photographs.

SERVICES:
Photocopying; microfiche reader. Limited parking
available.

SEE ALSO: NORTH EASTERN EDUCATION AND LIBRARY
BOARD, Ballymena

BALLYCONNELL BRANCH LIBRARY
SEE CAVAN COUNTY COUNCIL BRANCH LIBRARIES, Cavan

BALLYJAMESDUFF BRANCH LIBRARY
SEE CAVAN COUNTY COUNCIL BRANCH LIBRARIES, Cavan

CAVAN COUNTY MUSEUM
Virginia Road
BALLYJAMESDUFF, COUNTY CAVAN

TELEPHONE: 049–44070; FAX: 049–44332

HOURS:
MON-FRI: 10:00 am–5:00 pm;
SAT: 10:00 am–1:00 pm, 2:00 pm–5:00 pm

ACCESS:
Publicly-funded museum whose exhibits are open to
public for an admission charge. Current fee is £2 per
person. A library/archives is planned. Handicapped
accessible. Apprx. 50% of the museum's objects/
artefacts are catalogued.

CONTACT PERSON: Dominic Egan, Museum Curator

DESCRIPTION:
Cavan County Museum opened in June 1996 in the
former St. Clare Convent. The Museum seeks to
document material culture in Cavan and neighbouring
districts in counties Meath, Westmeath, Longford,
Leitrim, Fermanagh and Monaghan. Its displays vary
widely, focusing not only on the past but also the present
and the future. In addition to its permanent holdings, the
Museum exhibits materials from the National Museum
of Ireland, the Ulster Folk and Transport Museum, the
Ulster Museum, and various other national and foreign
institutions. The Museum includes exhibits on famous
citizens of the area, some of whom made their mark in
the New World.

SPECIAL COLLECTIONS:
The "Pighouse Collection," so named because it was
previously housed in a pighouse, was formed by Mrs.
Phyllis Faris and consists of a wide variety of material
on the life, history, customs and traditions of people in
County Cavan and the surrounding area.

SERVICES:
Brochures; flyers; ample free parking.

PUBLICATIONS:
The Museum is planning a publications program

SEE ALSO:
ARMAGH COUNTY MUSEUM, Armagh; NORTH DOWN
HERITAGE CENTRE, Bangor; ULSTER MUSEUM, Belfast;
TOWER MUSEUM, Derry; DOWN COUNTY MUSEUM;
Downpatrick; ENNISKILLEN CASTLE, Enniskillen; ULSTER
FOLK AND TRANSPORT MUSEUM, Cultra; DONEGAL COUNTY
MUSEUM, Letterkenny; IRISH LINEN CENTRE AND LISBURN
MUSEUM, Lisburn; MONAGHAN COUNTY MUSEUM,
Monaghan; and ULSTER-AMERICAN FOLK PARK, Omagh.

AREA LOCAL HISTORY COLLECTION
SEE AREA REFERENCE LIBRARY, Ballymena

AREA REFERENCE LIBRARY
Demesne Avenue
BALLYMENA, BT43 7BG

TELEPHONE: 01266–41531; FAX: 01266–46680

HOURS:
MON, TH: 9:30 am–8:00 pm;
TUE, WED: 9:30 am–5:30 pm;
FRI: 9:30 am–6:00 pm;
SAT: 9:30 am–1:00 pm

ACCESS:
Visitors welcome, but identification required. Borrowing
privileges for visitors may be restricted. Consult with
Librarian.

CONTACT PERSON: Mrs. P. Lane, Area Reference
Librarian

SERVICES:
Also houses AREA LOCAL HISTORY COLLECTION (contact
Mrs. L. Buick, Area Local Studies Librarian).

SEE ALSO: NORTH EASTERN EDUCATION AND LIBRARY
BOARD, Ballymena

BALLYMENA BRANCH LIBRARY
25-31 Demesne Avenue
BALLYMENA, BT43 7BG

TELEPHONE: 01266–41531

HOURS:
MON, TH, FRI: 10:00 am–8:00 pm;
TUE, WED: 10:00 am–5:30 pm;
SAT: 10:00 am–5:00 pm

ACCESS:
Visitors welcome, but identification required. Borrowing privileges for visitors may be restricted. Consult with Librarian.

CONTACT PERSON: Mrs. M. Bryson, District Librarian in charge

SERVICES:
Photocopying; microfiche reader; public car park nearby.

SEE ALSO: NORTH EASTERN EDUCATION AND LIBRARY BOARD, Ballymena

CENTRAL DIVISIONAL LIBRARY HEADQUARTERS
Demesne Avenue
BALLYMENA, BT43 7BG

TELEPHONE: 01266–41531; FAX: 01266–46680

HOURS:
MON–FRI: 9:00 am–1:00 pm, 1:45 pm–5:00 pm

ACCESS:
By appointment

CONTACT PERSON: Mr. M. McQuitty, Divisional Librarian

SEE ALSO: NORTH EASTERN EDUCATION AND LIBRARY BOARD, Ballymena

LOCAL GOVERNMENT LIBRARY COUNTY HALL
182 Galgorm Road
BALLYMENA, BT42 1HL

TELEPHONE: 01266–653333

HOURS:
MON–FRI: 9:00 am–1:00 pm

ACCESS:
Visitors welcome, but identification required. Borrowing

privileges for visitors may be restricted. Consult with Librarian.

CONTACT PERSON: Mrs. F. Magill, Senior Library Assistant in charge

SEE ALSO: NORTH EASTERN EDUCATION AND LIBRARY BOARD, Ballymena

NORTH EAST INSTITUTE
BALLYMENA CAMPUS
Trostan Avenue
BALLYMENA, BT43 7BN

TELEPHONE: 01266–664261; FAX: 01266–659245

HOURS:
MON–TH: 9:00 am–9:00 pm;
FRI: 9:00 am–4:30 pm

ACCESS:
Open to students of the Institute. Visitors may use the resources for reference purposes only. Printed catalogue and magazine article index. Collection available at two sites, the Farm Lodge Site and the Trostan Avenue Site.

CONTACT PERSON: Sam Bell, Curriculum and Learning Support Officer

DESCRIPTION:
Library of 10,000 volumes is used to support the curriculum of this Further Continuing Education Institute. Collection deals mainly with vocational interests, e.g., Social Care, Construction, Engineering, Catering, Hairdressing, Computing. Part of NEELB.

SERVICES:
Photocopying.

SEE ALSO: NORTH EASTERN EDUCATION AND LIBRARY BOARD, Ballymena

NORTH EASTERN EDUCATION AND
LIBRARY BOARD
LIBRARY SERVICE HEADQUARTERS
Demesne Avenue
BALLYMENA, BT43 7BG

TELEPHONE: 01266–664100; FAX: 01266–632038

HOURS:
MON–FRI: 9:00 am–1:00 pm, 1:45 pm–5:00 pm

ACCESS:
By appointment

CONTACT PERSON: Mrs. Pearl Valentine, Chief Librarian

DESCRIPTION:
NEELB is one of five such administrative boards in
Northern Ireland that oversee branch, school, special,
and mobile libraries within its region. NEELB is
responsible for 37 branch libraries (AHOGHILL, ANTRIM,
BALLEE, BALLYCASTLE, BALLYCLARE, BALLYMENA,
BALLYMONEY, BELLAGHY, BROUGHSHANE, BUSHMILLS,
CARNLOUGH, CARRICKFERGUS, CASTLEROCK, CLOGHMILLS,
CLOUGHFERN, COLERAINE, CRUMLIN, CULLEYBACKEY,
CUSHENDALL, DRAPERSTOWN, GARVAGH, GLENGORMLEY,
GREENISLAND, GREYSTONE, KILREA, LARNE, MAGHERA,
MAGHERFELT, MONKSTOWN, PORTGLENONE, PORTRUSH,
PORTSTEWART, RANDALSTOWN, RATHCOOLE, RATHLIN,
TEMPLEPATRICK, and WHITEHEAD), 3 special libraries, and
eight mobile libraries, plus group headquarters at
Antrim, Ballymena, Carrickfergus, Coleraine and
Magherafelt. NEELB Branch Libraries are listed under
city or town.

SERVICES:
Stocks large collection of library materials, which it
circulates to the various branch, special and mobile
libraries within its jurisdiction; provides special services
through its special libraries and mobile libraries.

SEE ALSO:
LOCAL GOVERNMENT LIBRARY, BALLYMENA; AREA
REFERENCE LIBRARY, Ballymena; IRISH ROOM, Coleraine.

BALLYMONEY BRANCH LIBRARY
Rodden Foot, Queen Street
BALLYMONEY, BT53 6JB

TELEPHONE: 012656–63589

HOURS:
TUE, TH: 10:30 am–1:00 pm, 2:00 pm–8:00 pm;
WED, FRI: 10:30 am–1:00 pm, 2:00 pm–5:30 pm;
SAT: 10:30 am–1:00 pm, 2:00 pm–5:00 pm

ACCESS:
Visitors welcome, but identification required. Borrowing

privileges for visitors may be restricted. Consult with Librarian. Handicapped accessible.

CONTACT PERSON: Miss. A. Maconaghie, Principal Library Assistant in charge

DESCRIPTION:
Small branch library with an educational and recreational reading collection. Also houses a modest local studies collection, with a special emphasis on Irish literature. The George Shiels Collection includes manuscripts, cards, photographs and letters belonging to the Ballymoney playwright.

SEE ALSO: NORTH EASTERN EDUCATION AND LIBRARY BOARD, Ballymena

BALLYNAHINCH BRANCH LIBRARY
Main Street
BALLYNAHINCH, BT24 8DN

TELEPHONE: 01238–566400

HOURS:
TUE, WED, TH: 10:00 am–1:00 pm, 2:00 pm–8:00 pm;
FRI, SAT: 10:00 am–1:00 pm, 2:00 pm–5:00 pm;
MON: CLOSED

ACCESS:
Visitors welcome, but identification required to borrow. Borrowing privileges for visitors may be restricted. Consult with Librarian. Handicapped accessible.

CONTACT PERSON: Mrs. Pamela Cooper, District Librarian

SEE ALSO: SOUTH EASTERN EDUCATION AND LIBRARY BOARD, Ballynahinch

LOCAL STUDIES COLLECTION
SOUTH EASTERN EDUCATION AND LIBRARY BOARD
Windmill Hill
BALLYNAHINCH, BT24 8DH

TELEPHONE: 01238–566400; FAX: 01238–565072

HOURS:
MON–FRI: 9:00 am–5:15 pm

ACCESS:
By appointment, advance notice preferable. Handicapped
access can be made available.

CONTACT PERSON: Mrs.B. Porter, Chief Librarian

DESCRIPTION:
The Local Studies Collection of the SEELB Library and
Information Service contains some unique material on
the history, literature and cultural development of
County Down and South Antrim. The collection of some
40,000 items includes photographs, postcards and
illustrations of the two counties, Ordnance Survey maps
and parish memoirs, and historic and contemporary
newspapers for the area.

SERVICES:
Publications; photocopying (b&w/col.); fax; online
access to Ulster-American Folk Park Emigration
Database; Internet; limited parking.

SEE ALSO: SOUTH EASTERN EDUCATION AND LIBRARY BOARD,
Ballynahinch

SAINTFIELD LIBRARY
Ballynahinch Road, Saintfield
BALLYNAHINCH, BT24 7AD

TELEPHONE: 01238–510550

HOURS:
TUE, TH.: 2:00 pm–8:00 pm;
FRI: 10:00 am–1:00 pm, 2:00 pm–5:00 pm;
SAT: 10:00 am–1:00 pm

ACCESS:
Visitors welcome, but identification required. Borrowing
privileges for visitors may be restricted. Consult with
Librarian.

CONTACT PERSON: Mrs. Pamela Macrory, Branch
Librarian

SEE ALSO: SOUTH EASTERN EDUCATION AND LIBRARY BOARD,
Ballynahinch

SOUTH EASTERN EDUCATION AND LIBRARY BOARD
LIBRARY HEADQUARTERS
Windmill Hill
BALLYNAHINCH, BT24 8DH

TELEPHONE: 01238–566400; FAX: 01238–565072

HOURS:
MON–FRI: 9:00 am–5:15 pm

ACCESS:
By appointment, with at least two days advance notice.
Handicapped access can be made available with
notification.

CONTACT PERSON: Mrs. B. Porter, Chief Librarian

DESCRIPTION:
One of five such administrative boards in Northern
Ireland, SEELB is charged with overseeing 26 branch
libraries (BALLYNAHINCH, BANGOR, BELVOIR, BRANIEL,
CARRYDUFF, CASTLEWELLAN, COMBER, CREGAGH, DAIRY
FARM, DONAGHADEE, DOWNPATRICK, DUNDONALD,
DUNMURRY, GILNAHIRK, HOLYWOOD, KILLYLEAGH,
LAURELHILL, LISBURN, MOIRA, NEWTOWNBREDA,
NEWCASTLE, NEWTOWNARDS, POLEGLASS, PORTAFERRY,
SAINTFIELD, and TULLYCARNET), plus school, special and
mobile libraries within its area, namely, County Down.

SERVICES:
SEELB holds 563,000 volumes in its library
headquarters and 26 branch libraries combined plus
significant collections of maps, microforms, recordings,
postcards and photographs. Ninety percent of the books
are catalogued online, and the remaining ten percent are
available on card catalogue. These collections are made
available through SEELB's branch and special libraries.
Special services are also made available to jails, prisons,
hospitals and homes.

SEE ALSO: LOCAL STUDIES COLLECTION, Ballynahinch

BALLYSHANNON BRANCH LIBRARY
SEE DONEGAL COUNTY LIBRARY ADMINISTRATIVE CENTRE,
Letterkenny

BANBRIDGE BRANCH LIBRARY
Scarva Road
BANBRIDGE, BT32 3AD

TELEPHONE: 01826–23973

HOURS:
MON, WED, FRI: 9:30 am–5:30 pm;
TUE, TH: 9:30 am–8:00 pm;
SAT: 9:30 am–5:00 pm

ACCESS:
Visitors welcome, but identification required. Borrowing
privileges for visitors may be restricted. Consult with
Librarian

CONTACT PERSON: Mrs. S. Scarlett, Branch Librarian

SEE ALSO: SOUTHERN EDUCATION AND LIBRARY BOARD,
Armagh

BANGOR BRANCH LIBRARY
80 Hamilton Road
BANGOR, BT20 4LH

TELEPHONE: 01247–270591; FAX: 01247–462744

HOURS:
MON, TUE, WED, FRI: 10:00 am–8:00 pm;
SAT: 10:00 am–1:00 pm, 2:00 pm–5:00 pm

ACCESS:
Visitors welcome, but identification required. Borrowing
privileges for visitors may be restricted. Consult with
Librarian. Handicapped access limited.

CONTACT PERSON: Miss Mary Bradley, Branch Librarian;
Miss Joan Barfoot, District Librarian

DESCRIPTION:
Busy branch library housing a collection of more than
28,000 volumes, mostly educational and recreational
reading, serving a population area of some 60,000 that
increases with summer vacationers. A good collection of
videos and recordings available.

SERVICES:
Photocopying; microfiche reader; brochures and
handouts; local flyers; public car parks nearby. Local
weekly newspaper, *The Co. Down Specatator,* available
on microfilm.

SEE ALSO: SOUTH EASTERN EDUCATION AND LIBRARY BOARD,
Ballynahinch

NORTH DOWN HERITAGE CENTRE
Town Hall, Castle Park Avenue
BANGOR, BT20 4BT

TELEPHONE: 01247–271200; FAX: 01247–271370

HOURS:
JULY–AUGUST:
TUE–SAT: 10:30 am–5:30 pm;
SUN: 2:00 pm–5:30 pm;
SEPTEMBER–JUNE:
TUE–SAT: 10:30 am–4:30 pm;
SUN: 2:00 pm–4:30 pm

ACCESS:
The Museum is open to the public, free of charge. The
Archives is open by prior arrangement only. Recognized
for its handicapped access. No flash photography
allowed. No empty bags may be taken into museum.
CONTACT PERSON: Ian Wilson, B.A., Dip.Ed., Heritage
Centre Manager

DESCRIPTION:
Museum founded "to reflect full archaeological,
historical, natural and cultural heritage of North Down."
Situated in refurbished buildings of the former stables of
Bangor Castle, built in 1852, the Museum features
historical exhibits focusing on the early Christian
period, Scottish settlers, and North Down's seaside
traditions. Audio-visual presentations complement
exhibits. Observation beehive in summer months.
Museum houses premier collection of photographs of
North Down area.

SPECIAL COLLECTIONS:
The Sir John Newell Jordan Collection of Far-Eastern
Objets d'art. Includes bronze and porcelain ware, an
ivory puzzle ball, lacquered and inlaid chests and
cabinets, and a stunning incense burner brought back to
Ireland at the turn of the century by the prominent
diplomat for whom the collection is named.

SERVICES:
Special exhibitions; wide range of leaflets and handouts;
photocopying; ample parking; restaurant; book shop;
operates out-centre at Cockle Row (seventeenth century

B

cottages), Groomsport, Co. Down.

SEE ALSO:
ARMAGH COUNTY MUSEUM, ARMAGH; CAVAN COUNTY
MUSEUM, Ballyjamesduff; ULSTER MUSEUM, Belfast;
ULSTER FOLK AND TRANSPORT MUSEUM, Cultra; TOWER
MUSEUM, Derry; DOWN COUNTY MUSEUM; Downpatrick;
ENNISKILLEN CASTLE, Enniskillen; IRISH LINEN CENTRE
AND LISBURN MUSEUM, Lisburn; DONEGAL COUNTY
MUSEUM, Letterkenny; MONAGHAN COUNTY MUSEUM,
Monaghan; and ULSTER-AMERICAN FOLK PARK, Omagh.

BELFAST:
(The SOUTH EASTERN EDUCATION AND LIBRARY BOARD,
Ballynahinch, maintains nine branch or special libraries
within the borders of Belfast but separate from the
jurisdiction of the BELFAST EDUCATION AND LIBRARY
BOARD. These SEELB libraries are listed alphabetically
following the listing for Branch libraries of the BELB.)

BELFAST EDUCATION AND LIBRARY
BOARD
BELFAST PUBLIC LIBRARIES
Royal Avenue
BELFAST, BT1 1EA

TELEPHONE: 01232–243233; FAX: 01232–332819

HOURS:
By appointment.

ACCESS:
By appointment.

CONTACT PERSON: J. N. Montgomery, Chief Librarian

DESCRIPTION:
The Belfast Education and Library Board is one of five
such administrative boards in Northern Ireland. It serves
as the umbrella organization for the Central Library,
Belfast and its twenty branch libraries as well as the
city's mobile, college and school libraries and specialists
departments. Together these libraries hold some
2,000,000 books and a wide range of non-book
materials.

SEE ALSO: CENTRAL LIBRARY, BELFAST AND BRANCH
LIBRARIES

CENTRAL LIBRARY, BELFAST
Royal Avenue
BELFAST BT1 1EA

TELEPHONE: 01232–243233; FAX: 01232–332819

HOURS:
MON, TH: 9:30 am–8:00 pm;
TUE, WED, FRI: 9:30 am–5:30 pm;
SAT: 9:30 am–1:00 pm

ACCESS:
Flagship library of the Belfast Education and Library
Board. Open to visitors for reference services but
borrowing privileges for non-residents may be restricted.
Consult with Librarian. Approximately 95% of the book
collection is catalogued – 20% in machine readable
form, 75% on cards. There are two printed catalogues.
About half the manuscript collection is catalogued on
cards. Stacks closed. Handicapped accessible.

CONTACT PERSONS: J. N. Montgomery, Chief Librarian;
Thomas Watson, Assistant Chief Librarian; Hugh
Russell, Senior Reference Librarian

DESCRIPTION:
The Central Library, opened in 1888, is an important
research library housing some 900,000 volumes of
books, the largest newspaper collection in Northern
Ireland, and significant holdings of periodicals,
manuscripts, maps, microforms, pamphlets,
photographs, postcards, music scores, recordings and
films. In addition to maintaining a strong general
collection and several major research collections, the
Library seeks to provide an up to date reference and
information service to the general public.

SPECIAL COLLECTIONS:
The Natural History Collection totals some 10,000
volumes. Assistant Chief Librarian Tom Watson took
special care to acquire copies in fine-to-mint condition,
and in 1988 he compiled an illustrated catalogue of
selected books from this collection. SEE PUBLICATIONS.
The Rare Books Collection includes a small but
excellent collection of incunabula and several hundred
pre-1701 English printed books, including a goodly
number of Popish Plot pamphlets. The Fine Press
holdings offer a good selection of the best modern

B

special presses, including a complete run of Cuala Press. The Irish Collection is the largest in NI, anchored by the 4,000-item Francis Joseph Bigger Collection. Bigger (1863-1926), the grandson of United Irishman David Bigger, was a successful lawyer and a member of the Gaelic League who assembled an impressive collection of books, pamphlets and bound manuscripts of Irish historical, archaeological and antiquarian interest. This collection was donated to the library by his brother Frederic in 1927, and a catalogue of 3,000 entries was published in 1930. Other major Irish holdings include some 800 pre-1851 Belfast imprints, an extensive collection of printed maps of Ireland, and several author collections, including manuscripts, e.g., Forrest Reid and Amanda McKittrick Ros. Complementing the Irish Collection is the newspaper library, which contains virtually complete runs of the *Belfast Telegraph, Newsletter, Irish News and Northern Whig*, plus extensive holdings of provincial papers from Ireland, north and south. The Library also houses the deposit collection of UK patents, a superb Music Library, and strong special holdings in the areas of the humanities, local history, business information, fine arts and literature and science and technology.

SERVICES:
Computerized, printed and card catalogues; photocopying and microfilming; brochures, handouts and guides, e.g. *Guide to Irish & Local Studies Department*; borrowing privileges by arrangement for visitors; bibliographies; city centre car parks nearby. The Library does not offer a genealogical service per se, but its holdings in this area are extensive, and staff are willing to assist researchers in so far as possible. Referrals are generally made to the PUBLIC RECORD OFFICE OF NORTHERN IRELAND, Belfast, and to THE GENERAL REGISTER OFFICE, Belfast.

PUBLICATIONS:
Annual Reports; Catalogue of Books and Bound Mss of the Irish Historical, Archaeological and Antiquarian Library of the Late Francis Joseph Bigger .... Belfast, 1930; [Watson, Thomas]. *Natural History: A Select List of Fine Books from the Stock of Belfast Central Library.* Belfast, 1988.

B

BRANCH LIBRARIES
BELFAST PUBLIC LIBRARIES

NOTE:
Branch Libraries are open to visitors, but borrowing
privileges may be restricted. Consult with Branch
Librarian. The 01232 Belfast city telephone code is not
needed if calling any of the following libraries from
within Belfast.

ANDERSONSTOWN
Slievegallion Drive
BELFAST, BT11 8JP

TELEPHONE: 301786

HOURS:
MON, TH: 1:30 pm–8:00 pm;
TUE, WED, FRI: 9:30 am–12:30 pm, 1:30 pm–5:30 pm;
SAT: 9:30 am–1:00 pm

ARDOYNE
446-450 Crumlin Road
BELFAST, BT14 7GH.

TELEPHONE: 391579

HOURS:
MON, TUE, WED, FRI: 9:30 am–1:00 pm, 2:00 pm–5:30 pm;
TH: 1:30 pm–7:00 pm;
SAT: 9:30 am–1:00 pm

BALLYHACKAMORE
1-3 Eastleigh Drive
BELFAST, BT4 3DX

TELEPHONE: 471387

HOURS:
MON, TH: 1:30 pm–8:00 pm;
TUE, WED, FRI: 9:30 am–5:30 pm;
SAT: 9:30 am–1:00 pm

BALLYMACARRETT
19-35 Templemore Avenue
BELFAST, BT5 4FP

TELEPHONE: 451533

HOURS:
MON, TH: 1:30 pm–8:00 pm;
TUE, WED, FRI: 9:30 am–5:30 pm;
SAT: 9:30 am–1:00 pm

CAIRNMARTIN
Mount Gilbert Community School
BELFAST, BT13 3NL

TELEPHONE: 712601

HOURS:
MON, WED, FRI: 1:30 pm–5:30 pm;
TUE, TH: 1:30 pm–8:00 pm

CHICHESTER
Salisbury Avenue
BELFAST, BT15 5EB

TELEPHONE: 370896

HOURS:
MON, TH: 1:30 pm–8:00 pm;
TUE, WED, FRI: 9:30 am–5:30 pm
SAT: 9:30 am–1:00 pm

FALLS ROAD
49 Falls Road
BELFAST, BT12 4PD

TELEPHONE: 326052

HOURS:
MON, TH: 1:30 pm–8:00 pm;
TUE, WED, FRI: 9:30 am–5:30 pm;
SAT: 9:30 am–1:00 pm

FINAGHY
Finaghy Road South
BELFAST, BT10 0BX

TELEPHONE: 301226

HOURS:
MON: 10:00 am–8:00 pm;
TUE, WED, FRI: 10:00 am–5:30 pm;
TH: 1:00 pm–8:00 pm

HOLYWOOD ARCHES
4-12 Holywood Road
BELFAST, BT4 1NT

TELEPHONE: 471309

HOURS:
MON, TH: 1:30 pm–8:00 pm;
TUE, WED, FRI: 9:30 am–5:30 pm;
SAT: 9:30 am–1:00 pm

LIGONIEL
53-55 Ligoniel Road
BELFAST, BT14 8BW

TELEPHONE: 391615

HOURS:
MON, TH: 1:30 pm - 8:00 pm;
TUE, WED, FRI: 9:30 am–12:30 pm, 1:30 pm–5:30 pm;
SAT: 9:30 am–1:00 pm

LISBURN ROAD
440 Lisburn Road
BELFAST, BT9 6GR

TELEPHONE: 381170

HOURS:
MON, TH: 1:30 pm–8:00 pm;
TUE, WED, FRI: 9:30 am–5:30 pm;
SAT: 9:30 am–1:00 pm

OLDPARK ROAD
46 Oldpark Road
BELFAST, BT14 6FS

TELEPHONE: 351591

HOURS:
MON: 1:30 pm–7:00 pm;
WED, FRI: 9:30 am–12:30 pm, 1:30 pm–5:30 pm

ORMEAU ROAD
Ormeau Road Embankment
BELFAST, BT7 3GG

TELEPHONE: 491591

HOURS:
MON, TH: 1:30 pm–8:00 pm;
TUE, WED, FRI: 9:30 am–5:30 pm;
SAT: 9:30 am–1:00 pm

SANDY ROW
127 Sandy Row
BELFAST, BT12 5ET

TELEPHONE: 326089

HOURS:
MON, TH: 1:30 pm–7:00 pm;
TUE, WED, FRI: 9:30 am–5:30 pm;
SAT: 9:30 am–1:00 pm

SHANKILL
298-300 Shankill Road
BELFAST, BT13 2BN

TELEPHONE: 326330

HOURS:
MON, TH: 1:30 pm–8:00 pm;
TUE, WED, FRI: 9:30 am–5:30 pm;
SAT: 9:30 am–1:00 pm

SKEGONEILL
Skegoneill Avenue
BELFAST, BT15 3JN

TELEPHONE: 370455

HOURS:
MON, TH: 1:30 pm–8:00 pm;
TUE, WED, FRI, 9:30 am–5:30 pm;
SAT: 9:30 am–1:00 pm

SUFFOLK
Stewartstown Road
BELFAST, BT11 9JP

TELEPHONE: 301183

HOURS:
MON, TH: 1:30 pm–8:00 pm;
TUE, WED, FRI: 9:30 am–5:30 pm;
SAT: 9:30 am–1:00 pm

WHITEROCK
Whiterock Road
BELFAST, BT12 7PG

TELEPHONE: 249846

HOURS:
MON, TH: 1:30 pm–8:00 pm;
TUE, WED, FRI: 9:30 am–5:30 pm

WHITEWELL
Ballygolan Primary School
BELFAST, BT36 7HB

TELEPHONE: 772677

HOURS:
MON: 2:00 pm–8:00 pm;
WED: 2:00 pm–5:00 pm;
FRI: 10:00 am–1:00 pm, 2:00 pm–5:00 pm

WOODSTOCK ROAD
358 Woodstock Road
BELFAST, BT6 9DQ

TELEPHONE: 732917

HOURS:
MON, TH: 1:30 pm–8:00 pm;
TUE, WED, FRI: 9:30 am–5:30 pm;
SAT: 9:30 am–1:00 pm

BELFAST LIBRARY AND SOCIETY FOR PROMOTING KNOWLEDGE
SEE LINEN HALL LIBRARY, Belfast

BELVOIR PARK LIBRARY
Drumart Square
BELFAST, BT8 4EY

TELEPHONE: 01232–644331

HOURS:
MON, FRI: 2:00 pm–8:00 pm;
TUE: 10:00 am–1:00 pm, 2:00 pm–5:00 pm;
SAT: 10:00 am–1:00 pm

ACCESS:
Visitors welcome, but identification required. Borrowing privileges for visitors may be restricted. Consult with Lbrarian.

CONTACT PERSON: Mrs. Joan Smith, Branch Librarian

SEE ALSO: SOUTH EASTERN EDUCATION AND LIBRARY BOARD, Ballynahinch

BRANIEL LIBRARY
Glen Road
BELFAST, BT5 7JH

TELEPHONE: 01232–797420

HOURS:
MON: 5:00 pm–8:00 pm;
TUE, FRI: 2:00 pm–5:00 pm;
WED: 10:00 am–1:00 pm, 2:00 pm–8:00 pm,
SAT: 10:00 am–1:00 pm

ACCESS:
Visitors welcome, but identification required. Borrowing privileges for visitors may be restricted. Consult with Librarian.

CONTACT PERSON: Mrs. Maisie Reid, Branch Librarian

SEE ALSO: SOUTH EASTERN EDUCATION AND LIBRARY BOARD, Ballynahinch

CREGAGH LIBRARY
409-413 Cregagh Road
BELFAST, BT6 0LF

TELEPHONE: 01232–401365

HOURS:
MON, TUE, TH: 10:00 am–8:00 pm;
FRI: 10:00 am–5:00 pm;
SAT: 9:00 am–1:00 pm

ACCESS:
Visitors welcome, but identification required. Borrowing

privileges for visitors may be restricted. Consult with
Librarian.

CONTACT PERSON: Miss Martha Anne Loan, Branch
Librarian; Miss Priscilla McMillen, District Librarian

SEE ALSO: SOUTH EASTERN EDUCATION AND LIBRARY BOARD,
Ballynahinch

DAIRY FARM LIBRARY
DAIRY FARM CENTRE, UNIT 17
Stewartstown Road, Dunmurry
BELFAST, BT17 0AW

TELEPHONE: 01232–431266; FAX: 01232–431278
HOURS:
MON, TUE: 9:30 am–5:30 pm;
WED, FRI: 1:00 pm–8:00 pm;
SAT: 9:30 am–1:00 pm, 2:00 pm–5:00 pm

ACCESS:
Visitors welcome, but identification required. Borrowing
privileges for visitors may be restricted. Consult with
Librarian.

CONTACT PERSON: Ms. Helen O'Hare, District Librarian

SEE ALSO: SOUTH EASTERN EDUCATION AND LIBRARY BOARD,
Ballynahinch

DIOCESAN LIBRARY OF DOWN AND
DROMORE AND CONNOR
CHURCH OF IRELAND HOUSE
61-67 Donegall Street
BELFAST, BT1 2QH

TELEPHONE: 01232–322268

HOURS:
By appointment

ACCESS:
The library is intended primarily for members of the
Church of Ireland doing research in theological studies.
Visitors welcome but application must be made in
advance during office hours to the Diocesan Office. Card
catalogue.

CONTACT PERSON: Mr. J.F. Rankin, Secretary to the
Library Committee

DESCRIPTION:
Primarily a theology and local church history library
originally established in 1854 and now located in the
new Diocesan centre at above address. The collection,
comprising some 1,000 volumes, plus pamphlets,
concentrates on theology, ecclesiastical and local church
history and law, and clerical and episcopal biographies.
Also includes some transcripts of Reeves, Reynell and
Leslie material. The Reeves archive relating to the
dioceses has been deposited with Public Record Office
of Northern Ireland.

SERVICES:
Photocopying

SEE ALSO: PUBLIC RECORD OFFICE OF NORTHERN IRELAND,
Belfast

DOWN & CONNOR DIOCESAN ARCHIVES
73a Somerton Road
BELFAST, BT15 4DJ

TELEPHONE: 01232–776185

HOURS:
By appointment

ACCESS:
Privately-funded archives of the Roman Catholic
Diocese of Down & Connor, which includes Belfast.
Advance notice required. Apply to Archivist.

CONTACT PERSON: Diocesan Archivist

DESCRIPTION:
Houses the official records of the Roman Catholic see of
Down & Connor. Of special interest are the
correspondence files of various bishops of the diocese
dating back to 1803.

SERVICES:
Photocopying.

SEE ALSO: ARMAGH DIOCESAN ARCHIVES, Armagh

DUNDONALD LIBRARY
16 Church Road, Dundonald
BELFAST, BT16 CLN

TELEPHONE: 01232–483994

HOURS:
MON, TUE, WED: 10:00 am–8:00 pm;
FRI: 10:00 am–5:00 pm;
SAT: 9:00 am–1:00 pm

ACCESS:
Visitors welcome, but identification required. Borrowing privileges available for visitors.

CONTACT PERSON: Mr. Diarmuid Kennedy, Manager

SEE ALSO: SOUTH EASTERN EDUCATION AND LIBRARY BOARD, Ballynahinch

EDGEHILL THEOLOGICAL COLLEGE
9 Lennoxvale
BELFAST, BT9 5BY

TELEPHONE: 01232–665870

HOURS:
SEPTEMBER–JUNE:
MON–FRI: 9:00 am–5:00 pm;
JULY–AUGUST:
Closed

ACCESS:
Theological library primarily for students and faculty of this Methodist college. Visitors welcome, but restrictions may apply. Consult with Librarian. Card catalogue.

CONTACT PERSON: Mrs. M. Gallagher, Librarian

DESCRIPTION:
Library of some 10,000 volumes, with special emphasis on theology and Methodism. Includes some rare material.

SERVICES:
Photocopying.

EUROPEAN BUSINESS INFORMATION CENTRE
LOCAL ENTERPRISE DEVELOPMENT UNIT (LEDU)
Ledhouse, Upper Galwally
BELFAST, BT8 4TB

TELEPHONE: 01232–491031; FAX: 01232–691432
E–MAIL: ebic.ledu@nics.gov.uk
WEB SITE: http://www.ledu–ni.gov.uk

HOURS:
MON–FRI: 9:00 am–5:00 pm

ACCESS:
Established to provide small businesses with access to a
unified European market, LEDU offers entrepreneurs
information resource services through its library
division. Library services are available to anyone
seeking to establish a business in Northern Ireland.

CONTACT PERSON: Eleanor Butterwick, Librarian

DESCRIPTION:
LEDU became a Euro Info centre in 1989. It maintains a
wide variety of resources, including trade directories,
environmental rules and regulations, and information on
standards, designed to encourage small business
development. Much of this information is in machine
readable form. The library does house, however, a
reference collection of about 2,000 volumes, plus
subscribes to some 250 periodicals.

SERVICES:
Photocopying, computerized searches, microfiche reader/
printer. LEDU maintains regional offices in Belfast,
Ballymena, Derry, Newtownards, Newry and Omagh.

FAMILIA: THE ULSTER HERITAGE CENTRE
SEE ULSTER HISTORICAL FOUNDATION, Belfast

GAMBLE LIBRARY
UNION THEOLOGICAL COLLEGE OF THE
PRESBYTERIAN CHURCH OF IRELAND
108 Botanic Avenue
BELFAST, BT7 1JT

TELEPHONE: 01232–325374, EXT. 23; FAX: 01232–325397

HOURS:
OCTOBER–JUNE:
MON: 10:00 am–4:30 pm;
TUE–WED: 9:00 am–4:30 pm;
TH–FRI: 9:00 am–4:00 pm;
SEPTEMBER:
TUE, TH: 9:00 am–4:00 pm;
Closed Saturdays, Sundays throughout the year, and the
months of July and August.

ACCESS:
The Library supports the work of the faculty, students of the college and ministers. Memberships are available on a fee basis. Consult with Librarian. Card catalogue.

CONTACT PERSON: Mrs. Doreen McDowell, Head Librarian

DESCRIPTION:
The collection of books exceeds 50,000 volumes, with a heavy focus on theology. A separate rare book collection features theology, linguistics, and church history. There are also record books of genealogical interest.

SERVICES:
Photocopying.

GENERAL REGISTER OFFICE
NORTHERN IRELAND STATISTICS AND RESEARCH AGENCY
Oxford House, 49–55 Chichester Street
BELFAST, BT1 4HL

TELEPHONE: 01232–252013; FAX: 01232–252044

HOURS:
MON–FRI: 9:30 am–4:00 pm;
Appointment preferred. Application and identification required. Handicapped accessible. General searches may be made by any member of the public over sixteen years of age, but a six-month advance reservation is required. Computerized indexes available from 1922 to present. NOTE: There are no general indexes for deaths and marriages before 1922 so it is necessary to know the district of registration.

ACCESS:
Open to the general public. Fees charged for searches and extracts. Current fees: Full certified birth, death or marriage certificate = £6.00; short birth certificate = £4.00; staff search for each five year period = £2.00; general searches by requester (up to six hours) = £6.00. NOTE: advance booking of 6-months required for general searches by requester.

CONTACT PERSON: J. L McKeag, Deputy Registrar General

DESCRIPTION:
The GRO Northern Ireland was opened in Belfast in

1922 following partition. Previously all records were kept at the GRO in Dublin, which was established in 1845. GRO NI houses vital records for the six counties of Northern Ireland for issue of certified copies to the public. These include birth, deaths, marriages, still-births and adoptions. Birth, death and Roman Catholic marriage registrations date from 1864 to the present; Protestant marriage from 1845 to the present; still-births from 1961 to the present; and adoptions from 1930 to the present.

SERVICES:
Certified copies of records; searches.

SEE ALSO: PUBLIC RECORD OFFICE OF NORTHERN IRELAND, Belfast

GILNAHIRK LIBRARY
Gilnahirk Rise
BELFAST, BT5 7DT

TELEPHONE: 01232–796573

HOURS:
TUE, TH: 4:00 pm–8:00 pm;
WED: 10:00 am–1:00 pm, 2:00 pm–5:00 pm;
SAT: 10:00 am–1:00 pm

ACCESS:
Visitors welcome, but identification required. Borrowing privileges for visitors may be restricted. Consult with Librarian.

CONTACT PERSON: Mrs. Lynn Rice, Branch Librarian

SEE ALSO: SOUTH EASTERN EDUCATION AND LIBRARY BOARD, Ballynahinch

INSTITUTE OF IRISH STUDIES
QUEEN'S UNIVERSITY, BELFAST
8 Fitzwilliam Street
BELFAST, BT9 6AW

TELEPHONE: 01232–273386; FAX: 01232–439238;
E–MAIL: irish.studies@qub.ac.uk

HOURS:
MON–FRI: 9:30 am–5:00 pm (closed 1:00 pm–2:00 pm)

ACCESS:
The Institute is an integral part of Queen's University and welcomes visiting scholars to use its facilities to further their writing and research. Appointment preferred.

CONTACT PERSONS: Professor Brian Walker, Director; Dr. Sophia M. King, Assistant Director

DESCRIPTION:
Established in 1965, the Institute seeks "to encourage interest and to promote and co-ordinate research in those fields of study which have particular Irish interest." The Institute takes a genuinely inter-disciplinary approach to its mission. Since 1987 the Institute has provided a B.A. degree in Irish Studies, a Master's degree and a Diploma course. The Institute sponsors an active seminar and publications program. The latter produces eight to ten new titles each year of an Irish academic interest, plus *The Irish Review*, a semi-annual interdisciplinary journal of Irish Studies.

SERVICES:
Staff provide advice on research subjects of an Irish interest. Ample opportunities for scholars to discuss work in progress. Services mostly aimed at scholarly research. Microfilm copies of original *Ordnance Survey Memoirs* available. The only other microfilm copy of the *Memoirs* is at the Royal Irish Academy in Dublin. Microfilm reader but no printer available.

SEE ALSO: QUEEN'S UNIVERSITY, Belfast

LEDU
SEE EUROPEAN BUSINESS INFORMATION CENTRE

LINEN HALL LIBRARY
(BELFAST LIBRARY AND SOCIETY FOR
PROMOTING KNOWLEDGE)
17 Donegall Square North
BELFAST, BT1 5GD

TELEPHONE: 01232–321707; FAX: 01232–438586

HOURS:
MON, TUE, WED, FRI: 9:30 am–5:30 pm;
TH: 9:30 am–8:30 pm (except July and August when
library closes at 5:30 pm);
SAT: 9:30 am–4:00 pm.
Closed week of July 12th

ACCESS:
Independent subscribing research library with some
public funding. Open to the public free of charge for
reference services. Borrowing privileges restricted to
members. General stacks open. Irish material stacks
closed. Handicapped access severely limited. Twenty
percent of the collection is catalogued in machine
readable form, 20% in printed catalogs, 40% on cards,
and 20% remains uncatalogued. Computerized
information services will be available in 1997.

CONTACT PERSON: John Gray, Librarian

DESCRIPTION:
The Linen Hall Library was founded in 1788 as the
Belfast Reading Society and is the oldest library in
Belfast. It is also the last surviving subscribing library in
Ireland. It is located on the upper two floors of a
nineteenth century warehouse in the City Centre, facing
City Hall. The library houses some 150,000 volumes,
75,000 pamphlets, plus significant holdings of
periodicals, newspapers, manuscripts, microforms and
photographs. It maintains a general lending and
reference collection, the latter being
especially strong in genealogy, heraldry, history and
travel. Its great strength, however, is its Irish and local
studies collection (Belfast, Antrim and Down), and the
Library seeks to collect comprehensively in these areas.

SPECIAL COLLECTIONS:
The Library's "Northern Ireland Political Collection"
contains some 80,000 items relating to the current
troubles, including runs of 1,500 periodical titles, 6,000
books, 3,000 posters, photographs and extensive
ephemera. The "Genealogical Collection" includes some
5,000 volumes, mainly of Ulster interest and Scottish
and American connections. Other significant collections
include the Kennedy Collection of Ulster Poetry, and
theatre and postcard collections.

SERVICES:
Catalogue access to most of the Library's holdings;
photocopying; fax; microfilm/fiche reader/printer;

brochures; city centre car parks nearby. Membership available immediately.

RESTRICTIONS:
References required for intensive access to Northern Ireland Political Collection. Computers and cameras can be used by arrangement. Bags cannot be left unattended.

BIBLIOGRAPHY:
Killen, John. *History of the Linen Hall Library* (Belfast, 1990); *The Linen Hall Review* (A biannual periodical that comes with membership); published *Annual Report*.

NEWTOWNBREDA LIBRARY
Saintfield Road
BELFAST, BT8 4HL

TELEPHONE: 01232–701620

HOURS:
MON, TUE, TH: 12:00 am–8:00 pm;
FR: 10:00 am–5:00 pm;
SAT: 9:00 am–1:00 pm

ACCESS:
Visitors welcome, but identification required. Borrowing privileges for visitors may be restricted. Consult with Librarian.

CONTACT PERSON: Mrs. Eileen Parker, Branch Librarian

SEE ALSO: SOUTH EASTERN EDUCATION AND LIBRARY BOARD, Ballynahinch

NORTHERN IRELAND ASSEMBLY LIBRARY
The Gate Lodge, Massey Avenue, Stormont Estate
BELFAST, BT4 2JT

TELEPHONE: 01232–521250; FAX: 01232–521715

HOURS:
MON–FRI: 9:05 am–5:15 pm

ACCESS:
Usually limited to government personnel. Referrals made to other appropriate sources. Some exceptions may be made. Appointment required. Apply in writing to Librarian, preferably with the sponsorship of an academic institution. Catalogue is being converted to machine readable form. Located in temporary quarters at

B

the Massey Avenue entrance to the Stormont Estate. Due to return to its home in the Parliament Building in 1997.

CONTACT PERSON: George D. Woodman, Librarian

DESCRIPTION:
Government library established in 1921 to provide library and reference assistance to members of the Parliament of Northern Ireland, renamed the Northern Ireland Assembly in 1973. Also acts as a reference service for Northern Ireland Government Departments, its primary mission since 1973. Collection exceeds 15,000 volumes, plus 60,000 official publications. Also contains modest holdings of journals, pamphlets, photographs. In addition to collecting Northern Ireland official publications and legislation, the Library focuses on Irish history and Northern Ireland history, government and politics. The Northern Ireland Collection emphasizes public administration, ethnic/religious conflict and constitutional law.

SPECIAL COLLECTIONS:
Collection of 18th century and earlier Irish historical and topographical materials; 18th century journals, acts and other Irish Parliamentary material.

SERVICES:
Short extracts may be copied; limited parking.

NORTHERN IRELAND HOUSING EXECUTIVE LIBRARY INFORMATION SERVICES
The Housing Centre, 2 Adelaide Street
BELFAST, BT2 8PB

TELEPHONE: 01232–318022; FAX: 01232–318024

HOURS:
MON–TH: 10:00 am–5:00 pm;
FRI: 10:00 am–4:00 pm

ACCESS:
Library primarily for use of staff. Visitors welcome to consult for reference purposes. Appointment required. Virtually entire collection catalogued in machine readable form. Stacks open.

CONTACT PERSON: Vivienne Halton, Library Information Officer

DESCRIPTION:
The Housing Executive administers a vast network of

public housing throughout Northern Ireland. Its library collection includes about 12,000 volumes and pamphlets plus some 200 periodical titles gathered to meet staff reference and research needs. Special interests include architecture and planning, construction, landscape design, housing, the public sector, management, finance and the social sciences, especially sociology. Also archives Housing Executive publications.

SERVICES:
Free photocopying; microfilm reader/printer; leaflets; restricted city centre parking.

ORDNANCE SURVEY OF NORTHERN IRELAND
Colby House, Stranmillis Court
BELFAST, BT9 5BJ

TELEPHONE: 01232–255755

HOURS:
MON–FRI: 9:15 am–4:30 pm

ACCESS:
By appointment
CONTACT PERSON: The Director

DESCRIPTION:
Archive houses significant holdings of maps and aerial films of Northern Ireland, including 6" county series maps, 1830-1900; 6" and 25" county series maps, 1900-1950; and Irish grid series maps at all scales and aerial films, 1959-onwards. OSNI is an Executive Agency with the Department of the Environment for Northern Ireland.

SERVICES:
Maps and photo prints can be purchased; search fees apply.

POLEGLASS LIBRARY
YOUTH & LIBRARY CENTRE
Good Shepherd Road, Poleglass
BELFAST, BT19 0LD

TELEPHONE: 01232–629740

HOURS:
MON, WED, TH: 2:00 pm–5:00 pm;

TUE: 10:00 am–1:00 pm, 2:00 pm–8:00 pm;
SAT: 10:00 am–1:00 pm

ACCESS:
Visitors welcome, but identification required. Borrowing
privileges for visitors may be restricted. Consult with
Librarian.

CONTACT PERSON: Mrs. Elizabeth McMullan, Branch
Librarian

SEE ALSO: SOUTH EASTERN EDUCATION AND LIBRARY BOARD,
Ballynahinch

PUBLIC RECORD OFFICE OF NORTHERN IRELAND
66 Balmoral Avenue
BELFAST, BT9 6NY

TELEPHONE: 01232–251318; FAX: 01232–255999;
E–MAIL: proni@nics.gov.uk
WEB SITE: http://proni.nics.gov.uk/index.htm

HOURS: MON–WED, FRI: 9:15 am–4:45 pm;
TH: 9:15–8:45 pm;
Closed two weeks in late November/early December.
Check in advance.

ACCESS:
Publicly-funded executive agency within the Department
of the Environment, open to the general public.
Identification required on arrival. Advance notice
preferred. There is no single printed guide to the records
held by PRONI, but there are exceptionally detailed
catalogues, indexes and finding aids to individual
collections. Consult with reference staff. Details of
acquisitions can be found in the annual *Deputy Keeper's
Reports*, indexed under personal names, places and
subjects. Though PRONI is the major resource for
genealogical information in Northern Ireland, it does not
carry out genealogical research of any kind for members
of the public. Staff will give guidance to visitors,
however. NOTE: Records generated by government and
other public bodies are generally not open to the public
until thirty years after the date of the last paper. This
period of closure may be extended for certain categories
of records, e.g., exceptionally sensitive papers,
documents containing information supplied in
confidence, and documents containing information about

individuals, the disclosure of which would cause distress or danger to living persons or their descendants.

CONTACT PERSON: Enquiries should be directed to the Readers Services Section

DESCRIPTION:
PRONI was established in 1923 following partition and opened in 1924 as the official repository for public records in Northern Ireland. It houses millions of documents, more than 53 shelf kilometres, the bulk of which deal with Northern Ireland since the early 1920s. The archive also includes older documents, some dating back to the 14th century, with strong holdings of material dating from 1600. Records fall into three major categories: records of government departments, some going back to the early 19th century; records of courts of law, local authorities and other non-departmental public bodies; and records deposited by private individuals, churches, businesses and institutions.

SPECIAL COLLECTIONS:
PRONI is a whole series of special collections. Categories: Records of Central and Local Government and Public Bodies; Tithe Applotment Records; Valuation Records, Maps, Plans and Surveys; Poor Law Records; School Records; Church Records (many available in a self-service microfilm facility); Landed Estate Records; Business Records; Solicitor's Records; Records of Private Individuals; and Photographic Records; PRONI also runs an Education and Conservation service. For more detail on each of these subject areas, refer to PRONI's Homepage on the Internet.

SERVICES:
Exhibits; photocopying; limited parking; restaurant.

PUBLICATIONS:
PRONI publishes a variety of books, exhibits catalogues, guides, facsimiles and finding aids to assist the user. These include the annual *Statutory Report* of the Deputy Keeper of the Records; *Guide to Sources for Women's History; Guide to Educational Records*; and various handouts on tracing your family tree. Publications can be ordered online.

SEE ALSO: GENERAL REGISTER OFFICE, BELFAST; QUEEN'S UNIVERSITY, Belfast

THE QUEEN'S UNIVERSITY OF BELFAST LIBRARY
University Road
BELFAST, BT7 1LS

TELEPHONE: 01232-335020; FAX: 01232-323340;
E-MAIL: qub.ac.uk

HOURS:
ACADEMIC YEAR (OCTOBER TO MID-JUNE): 9:00 am—10:00 pm;
VACATION: 9:00 am—5:00 pm;
SPECIAL COLLECTIONS:
ACADEMIC YEAR: MON–FRI: 9:00 am—9:30 pm;
VACATION: MON–FRI: 9:00 am—5:00 pm

ACCESS:
Publicly-funded academic research library open to the general public for reference purposes. Borrowing privileges may be extended to visitors for a fee. Consult with Librarian. Application to use special collections and the departmental libraries*; i.e., Agricultural and Food Science Library, Veterinary Science Library, Medical Library, and the Science Library, should be made in advance. Identification required. Special access rules apply for each of these units. For SPECIAL COLLECTIONS, application letter should include list of specific collections to be consulted, time of visit, and a letter of reference. Seating in special collections is very limited, and advance notice is essential. Most of the Library is handicapped accessible, including Special Collections. The entire book collection is catalogued in machine readable form using the LC classification system. Printed manuscripts catalogue.

CONTACT PERSON: Norman J. Russell, Librarian; Mary Kelly, Assistant Librarian for Special Collections

*Separate listings are not made in this guide for Queen's departmental libraries. These are located outside the main library and may be contacted directly as follows:
AGRICULTURAL AND FOOD SCIENCE LIBRARY, Agriculture & Food Science Centre, Newforge Lane, Belfast, BT9 5PX, Telephone: 01232-255227, Fax: 01232-255400;
VETERINARY SCIENCE LIBRARY, Veterinary Research Laboratories, Stormont, Belfast, BT4 3SD, Telephone: 01232-760011, ext. 222; MEDICAL LIBRARY, Institute of Clinical Science, Grosvenor Road, Belfast 12, Telephone: 01232-322043 / 321487; SCIENCE LIBRARY, 19 Chlorine Gardens, Belfast, BT 9 5EQ, Telephone: 01232-661111.

B

DESCRIPTION:
Queen's College, Belfast was established in Ireland by
Queen Victoria in 1845, along with colleges in Cork and
Galway. In 1908 it was elevated to University rank with
its own Charter and Statutes. Today the University
enrolls more than 13,000 full and part-time students.
The Library contains some 1,000,000 volumes plus
significant holdings of pamphlets, manuscripts, journals,
and microforms. It is the largest collection in Northern
Ireland. The collection is quite diverse, representing the
teaching and research interests of the curriculum and
faculty, but Irish studies is given special attention.

SPECIAL COLLECTIONS:
The Special Collections Department houses some 45,000
volumes, including 20 incunabula, manuscript
collections and the archives of the University. Major
individual collections include the Hibernica Collection;
the Sir Thomas Percy Collection, the 18th century
library of this Church of Ireland bishop of Dromore; the
Edward Bunting manuscript collection; the Thomas
Andrews, 1828-1876 and the James Thompson, 1857-
1892 collections of scientific papers; the Somerville and
Ross manuscript collection; Antrim Presbytery Library
of Theology; and the Robert Hart (1835-1911)
manuscript collection of Far Eastern materials, including
diaries and letters. Hart, a native of Lisburn, was
Inspector General of Maritime Customs in China from
1868 to 1907.

RESTRICTIONS:
For SPECIAL COLLECTIONS: Closed stacks; pencils only;
permission required for use of camera and computer.
Limited electric outlets restrict use of computers.
Battery-operated computers desirable. Photocopying
done by staff only.

PUBLICATIONS:
See T.W. Moody and J. C. Beckett, *Queen's Belfast*
(1959); and B. M. Walker and A. McCreary, *Degrees of
Excellence* (1994).

SERVICES:
Exhibits; photocopying; microfilm reader/printer;
published guides.

SEE ALSO:
GENERAL REGISTER OFFICE, BELFAST; INSTITUTE OF IRISH
STUDIES, Belfast; PUBLIC RECORD OFFICE OF NORTHERN
IRELAND, Belfast

ROYAL COLLEGE OF NURSING LIBRARY
SEE VIRGINIA HENDERSON LIBRARY, BELFAST

ST. MALACHY'S COLLEGE DIOCESAN LIBRARY
36 Antrim Road
BELFAST, BT15 2AE

TELEPHONE: 01232–748285; FAX: 01232–741066
E–MAIL: st.se@campus.bt.com

HOURS:
By appointment

ACCESS:
Roman Catholic secondary school. Visitors welcome to consult the library holdings, but materials cannot be taken from the library. Application in advance required. Card catalogue. No handicapped access.

CONTACT PERSON: G.J. McNamee, Archivist

DESCRIPTION:
St. Malachy's College houses an extensive collection of antiquarian books, about 8,000 in all, mostly on theology, classics, science, philosophy and history, especially Irish history, largely assembled by Mgr. James O'Laverty, author of the five-volume *Historical Account of the Diocese of Down and Connor Ancient and Modern* (1878-1895). The library also houses the school's archives, including memoirs, diaries, photographs and lists of former students and staff. The archives also include 16 Gaelic manuscripts collected by O'Laverty (d.1906), and cuttings and notes of Laurence O'Neill, Lord Mayor of Dublin, 1918-1924.

SEE ALSO: DOWN AND CONNOR DIOCESAN ARCHIVES, Belfast.

ST. MARY'S COLLEGE LIBRARY
191 Falls Road
BELFAST, BT12 6FE

TELEPHONE: 01232–327678; FAX: 01232–333719

HOURS:
TERM: MON–FRI: 9:00 am–9:00 pm;
VACATION: MON-FRI: 9:00 am–1:00 pm, 2:00 pm–5:00 pm

ACCESS:
One of two publicly-funded education colleges in

Northern Ireland open to the general public for reference purposes. Visitors welcome, especially out of term, but borrowing privileges may be restricted. Consult with Librarian. Advance notice preferred. Identification required. Over half of the collection is catalogued in machine readable form, the balance on cards. Open stacks. Handicapped accessible.

CONTACT PERSON: Sheila Fitzpatrick, Librarian

DESCRIPTION:
St. Mary's College prepares teachers who are committed to the Catholic vision of education in Northern Ireland. It was founded in 1900 by the Dominican Sisters to educate young women for the Catholic school system. In 1985, St. Mary's amalgamated with St. Joseph's, the Catholic men's college, to form the present St. Mary's. Its library supports the learning, teaching and research needs of staff and students. The collection includes some 87,000 volumes, 325 journals and a good collection of pamphlets, tapes, slides and videos. Areas of chief interest are: Education; Irish Studies; Religious Education; Theology; and Children's Literature, including material in Irish.

SPECIAL COLLECTIONS:
Official Catholic Church documents

SERVICES:
Photocopying; microfilm/fiche reader/printer; Internet access; finding aids; printed guide.

SEE ALSO: STRANMILLIS COLLEGE, Belfast.

STRANMILLIS COLLEGE LIBRARY
BELFAST, BT9 5DY

TELEPHONE: 01232–381309; FAX: 01232–663682;
E–MAIL: libaray@stran–ni.ac.uk;
WEB SITE: http://www.stran–ni.ac.uk/

HOURS:
TERM: MON–TH: 9:00 am–9:00 pm;
FRI: 9:00 am–4:30 pm;
VACATION: MON–TH: 9:00 am–5:00 pm;
FRI: 9:00 am–4:30 pm

ACCESS:
One of two publicly-funded education colleges in Northern Ireland open to the general public for reference

purposes. Visitors welcome, especially out of term, but borrowing privileges may be restricted. Consult with Librarian. Advance notice preferred. Identification required. Four-fifths of the collection is catalogued in machine readable form, the balance on cards. Open stacks. Handicapped accessible by arrangement.

CONTACT PERSON: Wesley McCann, Librarian

DESCRIPTION:
Stranmillis was founded in 1922 following partition as a training college for teachers. It is located on a beautiful campus in South Belfast, two miles from City Centre on the Stranmillis Road. Today it concentrates on preparing teachers who work with ages 3 to 13. Its library supports the learning, teaching and research needs of staff and students. The collection includes some 90,000 volumes, and 400 journal titles. Areas of chief curricular interest are: Education; English; Religious Studies; History; Art; Design and Technology; Science; French; Geography; Physical Education; Music and Drama.

SPECIAL COLLECTIONS:
Ulster collection of books relating to the northern counties of Ireland; modest collection of 19th century Irish school books; microfilm of *Belfast News Letter*, 1737-1925; and a microfilm of the Lawrence collection of Irish photographs, 1880-1914, the original located at the National Library of Ireland.

SERVICES:
Photocopying; microfilm/fiche reader/printer; computerized databases; finding aids; printed guide; parking by arrangement.

SEE ALSO: ST. MARY'S COLLEGE LIBRARY, Belfast.

TULLYCARNET LIBRARY
Kinross Avenue
BELFAST, BT5 7GF

TELEPHONE: 01232-485079; FAX: 01232-482342;
E-MAIL: tcarnet.maada@dnet.co.uk

HOURS:
MON, TUE, TH: 10:00 am–6:00 pm;
FRI: 10:00 am–5:00 pm;
SAT: 9:00 am–1:00 pm

ACCESS:
Visitors welcome, but identification required. Borrowing
privileges available for visitors. Handicapped accessible.

CONTACT PERSON: Mrs. Vivien Marshall, Branch Library
Manager; Ms. Adrienne Adair, District Library Manager

DESCRIPTION:
Main music library for the SEELB, sponsoring music
recitals, art and craft exhibitions throughout the year.

SERVICES:
Community Information Technology Point (access to
computers and the Internet for unwaged adults; Adult
storytelling monthly.

SEE ALSO: SOUTH EASTERN EDUCATION AND LIBRARY BOARD,
Ballynahinch

ULSTER CANCER FOUNDATION
40–42 Eglantine Avenue
BELFAST, BT9 6DX

TELEPHONE: 01232–663281; FAX: 01232–660081

HOURS:
MON–FRI: 9:00 am–12:30 pm, 2:00 pm–5:00 pm
Appointment preferred

ACCESS:
Open to the general public. Visitors welcome, but
advance notice is preferred, and there is an application
procedure.

CONTACT PERSON: Ms. Arlene Spiers, Head of
Community Services

DESCRIPTION: Library houses a small, general reference
collection designed to provide public and health
professionals with information on cancer related topics.

SERVICES:
Reference assistance; photocopying; brochures; school
teaching packs.

ULSTER HISTORICAL FOUNDATION
Balmoral Buildings, 12 College Square East
BELFAST, BT1 6DD

TELEPHONE: 01232–332288; FAX: 01232–239885
E–MAIL: enquiry@uhf.dnet.co.uk; WEB SITE: http://www.uhf.org.uk

HOURS:
By appointment. Preliminary inquiry in writing preferred. UHF also operates an adjacent retail outlet, FAMILIA: THE ULSTER HERITAGE CENTRE that specializes in Irish family and local history books, maps, crafts and related material.

NORMAL BUSINESS HOURS
MON–FRI: 9:00 am–5:00 pm;
There is a walk through facility from the Centre to UHF's offices in operation for visitors who wish to avail themselves of the Foundation's ancestral research service.

ACCESS:
Publicly and privately-funded not-for-profit genealogical research centre and publisher, open to the public. Research consultancy provided for a fee, currently £10 per half hour session. Preliminary search assessments, carried out for a fee, currently £15. For schedule of research fees, contact Secretary (or view Web site).

CONTACT PERSON: Shane McAteer, Secretary.

DESCRIPTION:
Located in Belfast city centre, the Ulster Historical Foundation is Ulster's principal genealogical research centre. Founded in 1956 to promote interest in Ulster history and genealogy, it provides a professional and comprehensive ancestral research service for the historic province of Ulster, publishes books and pamphlets, and organizes annual family history and heritage conferences. It is a member of the Irish Genealogical Project, a country-wide effort to computerize all the major Irish genealogical sources. To this end, it has been at work for years compiling a comprehensive computerized database of genealogical records for Ulster, principally for Counties Antrim and Down, including Belfast. This database is used as a tool, in conjunction with other documentary sources, to provide a comprehensive ancestral research service. Database contains: Pre-1900 church and civil records for counties Antrim and Down, including Belfast, plus gravestone transcripts for most of Northern Ireland. The Foundation also publishes a wide range of materials, primarily in the areas of Irish, local and family history.

SPECIAL COLLECTIONS:
Collection of some 8,000 family history reports carried out by UHF since 1956.

SERVICES:
Research; photocopying; information pack; book shop;
public car park nearby.

SEE ALSO:
ARMAGH ANCESTRY, Armagh; CAVAN GENEALOGICAL
RESEARCH CENTRE, Cavan; THE GENEALOGY CENTRE,
Derry; HERITAGE WORLD, Dungannon; MONAGHAN
ANCESTRY, Monaghan; and DONEGAL ANCESTRY,
Ramelton. Also: GENERAL REGISTER OFFICE, Belfast; and
the PUBLIC RECORD OFFICE OF NORTHERN IRELAND, Belfast.

ULSTER MUSEUM
Botanic Gardens
BELFAST, BT9 5AB

TELEPHONE: 01232–383000; FAX: 01232–383003

HOURS:
MON–FRI: 10:00 am–5:00 pm;
SAT: 1:00 pm–5:00 pm;
SUN: 2:00 pm–5:00 pm

ACCESS:
Open to the public, free of charge. Certain special
exhibitions may involve a fee. Handicapped accessible

CONTACT PERSON: Museum Director

DESCRIPTION:
Located next to the Botanic Gardens and the Queen's
University, this is the flagship of the museum system in
Northern Ireland. In addition to strong holdings of fine
and decorative art, including a representative collection
of Irish painting and sculpture from the late 17th century
to the present, the museum houses important collections
of botany and zoology, archaeology and ethnography,
geology and local history. Permanent displays include:
The Dinosaur Show; Making Irish Linen; Made in
Belfast; Mediaeval Ireland; Armada Treasures; The
Geology of Ireland; Irish Flora and Fauna; Costume and
Textiles; and Decorative Arts. NOTE: An administrative
merger of the three main museums, the Ulster-American
Folk Park, the Ulster Folk and Transport Museum, and
the Ulster Museum, is being planned. The word "Ulster"
may be dropped from the title of the new, merged
institution.

SPECIAL COLLECTIONS:
Collection of material excavated from the wrecks of
three Spanish Armada ships that foundered off the Irish
coast; Irish antiquities; British and Irish paintings and
sculptures. See also library holdings below.

SERVICES:
Exhibits; leaflets; shop, cafe.

SEE ALSO:
ULSTER MUSEUM LIBRARY, Belfast. Also, ARMAGH COUNTY
MUSEUM, Armagh; CAVAN COUNTY MUSEUM,
Ballyjamesduff; NORTH DOWN HERITAGE CENTRE, Bangor;
ULSTER FOLK AND TRANSPORT MUSEUM, Cultra; TOWER
MUSEUM, Derry; DOWN COUNTY MUSEUM; Downpatrick;
ENNISKILLEN CASTLE, Enniskillen; DONEGAL COUNTY
MUSEUM; Letterkenny; IRISH LINEN CENTRE AND LISBURN
MUSEUM, Lisburn; MONAGHAN COUNTY MUSEUM,
Monaghan; and ULSTER-AMERICAN FOLK PARK, Omagh.

ULSTER MUSEUM LIBRARY
Botanic Gardens
BELFAST, BT9 5AB

TELEPHONE: 01232–383000, EXT. 240; FAX: 01232–383003

HOURS:
MON–FRI: 9:00 am–12:45 pm, 2:00 pm–5:00 pm

ACCESS:
Collection is designed primarily for use of museum staff
but public welcome by appointment. Non-circulating
collection, but see SERVICES below. Card catalogue.

CONTACT PERSON: Registrar

DESCRIPTION:
Library contains approximately 37,000 volumes and
maintains about 200 current periodical titles. There is
also a small document archives and a collection of some
15,000 photographic negatives. Subjects covered include
archaeology, ethnology, art, botany, conservation, design,
geology, industrial archaeology, local history, museology,
numismatics, photography, zoology and general
reference.

SPECIAL COLLECTIONS:
Belfast printed books, (1700-1850); various manuscript
collections relating to local naturalists, e.g., botanist

John Templeton (1766-1825); photographer and
naturalist Robert J. Welch (1859-1936); R. J. Welch
Collection of photographic negatives (5,000 items); Alex
R. Hogg Collection of photographic negatives and
lantern slides (6,000 items).

SERVICES:
Reference services. Items may be lent to staff, other
libraries and accredited research workers. Consult with
registrar.

SEE ALSO: ULSTER MUSEUM, Belfast

UNIVERSITY OF ULSTER AT BELFAST
FACULTY OF ART & DESIGN LIBRARY
York Street
BELFAST, BT15 1ED

TELEPHONE: 01232-267269; FAX: 01232-267278;
E–MAIL: o.fitzpatrick@ulst.ac.uk

HOURS:
TERM: MON–TH: 9:OO am–10:00 pm;
FRI: 9:00 am–6:00 pm;
SAT: 10:00 am–1:00 pm;
VACATION: MON–TH: 9:00 am–5:00 pm;
FRI: 9:00 am–4:30 pm

ACCESS:
Academic library, part of the four-campus University of
Ulster system. Visitors welcome, but advance notice is
preferred and identification required. On this campus of
the University borrowing privileges are not extended to
visitors. Collection catalogued in machine readable
form, with about a 10% backlog of uncatalogued
material. The catalogue integrates the holdings of all
four libraries of the University. Handicapped accessible
with some restrictions.

CONTACT PERSON: Ms. Olivia Fitzpatrick, Sub-Librarian;
Ms. Nicky-Sinead Gardner, Director of Educational
Services.

DESCRIPTION:
Located in Belfast city centre, the Belfast campus is part
of the four-campus University of Ulster system. It
originated as a technical college and was established as
a University Faculty in 1984, concentrating on art and
design mainly at the undergraduate level. Its library of

some 40,000 volumes and more than 70,000 slides supports the campus's curriculum, with strengths in the areas of fine art, design, graphics, fashion, textiles, ceramics, jewelry, metal work, architecture, film, photography and print making. The Library regularly sponsors important exhibitions related to its holdings/ interests, e.g., "The Wood Engravings of Robert Gibbings" (1988); "Illustrated by Hugh Thomson, 1860-1920" (1989); "The Dolmen Press, 1951-1987" (1991) and "Wendy Dunbar: Book Designer" (1994). An illustrated catalogue was produced for each of these exhibitions.

SPECIAL COLLECTIONS:
Collection of slides of Belfast political wall murals

SERVICES:
Exhibitions; reference assistance; photocopying (b/w and colour); computerized databases online and CD-ROM; brochures and printed guides.

SEE ALSO:
UNIVERSITY OF ULSTER AT COLERAINE, Coleraine;
UNIVERSITY OF ULSTER, MAGEE COLLEGE, Derry; and
UNIVERSITY OF ULSTER AT JORDANSTOWN, Jordanstown

VIRGINIA HENDERSON LIBRARY
ROYAL COLLEGE OF NURSING
17 Windsor Avenue
BELFAST, BT9 6EE

TELEPHONE: 01232–668236; FAX: 01232–382188

HOURS:
TERM: MON–WED: 9:00 am–7:00 pm;
TH–FRI: 9:00 am–4:45 pm;
VACATION: MON–FRI: 9:00 am–4:45 pm

ACCESS:
Special library for members of the Royal College of Nurses. Visitors welcome on prior application. Identification required, with proof of bone fide membership in nursing organization. No charge. Not fully handicapped accessible. Collection catalogued on database.
CONTACT PERSON: Ms. M. Dwyer, Librarian

DESCRIPTION:
Library of some 6,500 volumes and 50 journal titles to

support the courses run by the Royal College of Nursing
Institute. Courses satisfy needs of R.C.N.
members in their continuing education and
personal development. Collection covers all
aspects of nursing and allied health issues. Use of
typewriters, computers, cameras or other items
that might disturb patrons restricted.

SERVICES:
Photocopying; literature searches.

BELLAGHY BRANCH LIBRARY
79 William Street
BELLAGHY, BT45 8HZ

TELEPHONE: 01648–386627

HOURS:
TUE, FRI: 2:00 pm–5:00 pm, 5:30 pm–7:30 pm;
WED: 10:30 am–1:00 pm, 2:00 pm–5:00 pm;
SAT: 10:00 am–1:00 pm, 2:00 pm–5:00 pm

ACCESS:
Visitors welcome, but identification required. Borrowing
privileges for visitors may be restricted. Consult with
Librarian.

CONTACT PERSON: Mrs. M. Jones, Senior Library
Assistant in charge

SEE ALSO: NORTH EASTERN EDUCATION AND LIBRARY
BOARD, Ballymena

BELTURBET BRANCH LIBRARY
SEE CAVAN COUNTY COUNCIL BRANCH LIBRARIES, Cavan

BESSBROOK BRANCH LIBRARY
Church Road
BESSBROOK, BT35 7AQ

TELEPHONE: 01693–830424

HOURS:
TUE: 2:00 pm–8:00 pm;
WED, FRI: 10:00 am–5:00 pm;
SAT. 11:00 am–3:30 pm

ACCESS:
Visitors welcome, but identification required. Borrowing privileges for visitors may be restricted. Consult with Librarian.

CONTACT PERSON: Mrs. A. Morgan, Mrs. M. Byrne

SEE ALSO: SOUTHERN EDUCATION AND LIBRARY BOARD, Armagh

BRONTE LIBRARY
SEE RATHFRILAND BRANCH LIBRARY

BROUGHSHANE BRANCH LIBRARY
Main Street
BROUGHSHANE, BT42 4JW

TELEPHONE: 01266–861613

HOURS:
TUE, FRI: 2:00 pm–5:00 pm, 6:00 pm–8:00 pm;
TH: 10:30 am–1:00 pm, 2:00 pm–5:30 pm;
SAT: 10:30 am–1:00 pm, 2:00 pm–5:00 pm

ACCESS:
Visitors welcome, but identification required. Borrowing privileges for visitors may be restricted. Consult with Librarian.

CONTACT PERSON: Mrs. F. Watson, Senior Library Assistant in charge

SEE ALSO: NORTH EASTERN EDUCATION AND LIBRARY BOARD, Ballymena

BUNCRANA BRANCH LIBRARY
SEE DONEGAL COUNTY LIBRARY ADMINISTRATIVE CENTRE, Letterkenny

BUNDORAN BRANCH LIBRARY
SEE DONEGAL COUNTY LIBRARY ADMINISTRATIVE CENTRE, Letterkenny

B

BUSHMILLS BRANCH LIBRARY
44 Main Street
BUSHMILLS, BT57 8QA

TELEPHONE: 012657–31424

HOURS:
TUE, WED: 10:30 am–1:00 pm, 2:00 pm–5:30 pm;
FRI: 10:30 am–1:00 pm, 2:00 pm–5:30 pm, 6:00 pm–7:00 pm;
SAT: 10:30 am–1:00 pm, 2:00 pm–5:00 pm

ACCESS:
Visitors welcome, but identification required. Borrowing privileges for visitors may be restricted. Consult with Librarian.

CONTACT PERSON: Mrs. Y Hill, Senior Library Assistant in charge

SEE ALSO: NORTH EASTERN EDUCATION AND LIBRARY BOARD, Ballymena

CARNDONAGH BRANCH LIBRARY

SEE DONEGAL COUNTY LIBRARY ADMINISTRATIVE CENTRE,
Letterkenny

CARNLOUGH BRANCH LIBRARY

Town Hall
CARNLOUGH, BT44 0EU

TELEPHONE: 01574–885552

HOURS:
TUE, FRI: 2:30 pm–5:00 pm, 5:30 pm–8:00 pm;
TH, SAT: 10:30 am–1:00 pm, 2:00 pm–5:00 pm

ACCESS:
Visitors welcome, but identification required. Borrowing
privileges for visitors may be restricted. Consult with
Librarian.

CONTACT PERSON: Mrs. M. Fyfe, Senior Library Assistant
in charge

SEE ALSO: NORTH EASTERN EDUCATION AND LIBRARY
BOARD, Ballymena

CARRICKFERGUS BRANCH LIBRARY

2 Joymount Court
CARRICKFERGUS, BT38 7DQ

TELEPHONE: 01960–362261; FAX: 01960–360589

HOURS:
MON, WED, FRI: 10:00 am–8:00 pm;
TUE, TH: 10:00 am–5:30 pm;
SAT: 10:00 am–5:00 pm

ACCESS:
Visitors welcome, but identification required. Borrowing
privileges for visitors may be restricted. Consult with
Librarian. More than ninety percent of the collection is
catalogued in machine readable form, the balance on
cards. Handicapped accessible.

CONTACT PERSON: Mr. A. J. Armstrong, District Librarian
in charge

DESCRIPTION:
Library opened in 1978 near Carrickfergus Castle, one of the best preserved Norman castles in Ireland. Library houses some 30,000 books and good collections of maps, videos and recordings. The Library features a local history room, focusing on Carrickfergus and Ireland. This collection of some 750 volumes, plus directories and journals, is especially good on county histories and Irish literature.

SERVICES:
Photocopying, video rental; brochures and leaflets; public car park nearby.

SEE ALSO: NORTH EASTERN EDUCATION AND LIBRARY BOARD, Ballymena

SOUTH DIVISIONAL LIBRARY HQ
2 Joymount Court
CARRICKFERGUS, BT38 7DQ

TELEPHONE: 01960–362261; FAX: 01960–360589

HOURS:
MON–FRI: 9:00 am–5:00 pm

ACCESS:
By appointment

CONTACT PERSON: Mr. M. McFaul, Divisional Librarian

DESCRIPTION:
Oversees and coordinates operations of branch libraries in the southern division within the jurisdiction of the North Eastern Education and Library Board.

SEE ALSO: NORTH EASTERN EDUCATION AND LIBRARY BOARD, Ballymena

CARRICKMACROSS BRANCH LIBRARY
Market Square
CARRICKMACROSS, COUNTY MONAGHAN

TELEPHONE: 042–61148

HOURS:
MON, FRI: 11:00 am–1:30 pm, 2:30 pm–5:00 pm, 6:00 pm–8:00 pm;
TUE, TH: 11:00 am–1:30 pm, 2:30 pm–5:00 pm

C

ACCESS:
Visitors welcome. Limited borrowing privileges available to visitors.

CONTACT PERSON: Senior Library Assistant

SEE ALSO: MONAGHAN COUNTY LIBRARY, Monaghan

CARRYDUFF LIBRARY
Church Road
CARRYDUFF, BT8 3DT

TELEPHONE: 012322–813568

HOURS:
MON, WED: 2:00 pm–8:00 pm;
FRI: 10:00 am–1:00 pm, 2:00 pm–5:00 pm;
SAT: 10:00 am–1:00 pm

ACCESS:
Visitors welcome, but identification required. Borrowing privileges for visitors may be restricted. Consult with Librarian.

CONTACT PERSON: Mrs. Patricia Ramsay, Branch Librarian

SEE ALSO: SOUTH EASTERN EDUCATION AND LIBRARY BOARD, Ballynahinch

CASTLEBLAYNEY BRANCH LIBRARY
Market Square
CASTLEBLAYNEY, COUNTY MONAGHAN

TELEPHONE: 042–40281

HOURS:
MON, FRI: 3:00 pm–5:00 pm, 6:00 pm–8:00 pm;
WED, TH: 12:00 pm–2:00 pm, 3:00 pm–5:00 pm

ACCESS:
Visitors welcome. Limited borrowing privileges available to visitors.

CONTACT PERSON: Senior Library Assistant

SEE ALSO: MONAGHAN COUNTY LIBRARY, Monaghan

CASTLEDERG BRANCH LIBRARY
Main Street
CASTLEDERG, BT81 7AY

TELEPHONE: 016626–71419

HOURS:
TUE: 1:00 pm–8:00 pm;
TH–FRI: 10:00 am–1:00 pm, 2:00 pm–5:30 pm;
SAT: 10:00 am–1:00 pm

ACCESS:
Visitors welcome, but identification required. Borrowing
privileges for visitors may be restricted. Consult with
Librarian. Collection totals apprx.7,000 volumes.

CONTACT PERSON: Mrs. T. Lecky

SEE ALSO: WESTERN EDUCATION AND LIBRARY BOARD,
Omagh

CASTLEROCK BRANCH LIBRARY
57 Main Street
CASTLEROCK, BT51 4RA

TELEPHONE: 01265–848463

HOURS:
TUE: 2:00 pm–5:30 pm, 6:00 pm–8:00 pm;
WED, FRI: 2:00 pm–5:30 pm;
SAT: 10:30 am–1:00 pm, 2:00 pm–5:00 pm

ACCESS:
Visitors welcome, but identification required. Borrowing
privileges for visitors may be restricted. Consult with
Librarian.

CONTACT PERSON: Mrs. G. Hanns, Senior Library
Assistant in charge

SEE ALSO: NORTH EASTERN EDUCATION AND LIBRARY
BOARD, Ballymena

CASTLEWELLAN BRANCH LIBRARY
Main Street
CASTLEWELLAN, BT31 9DA

TELEPHONE: 013967–78433

HOURS:
MON, WED: 2:00 pm–8:00 pm;
FRI: 10:00 am–1:00 pm, 2:00 pm–5:00 pm;
SAT: 10:00 am–1:00 pm

ACCESS:
Visitors welcome, but identification required. Borrowing privileges for visitors may be restricted. Consult with Librarian. Collection catalogued in machine readable form. Handicapped accessible.

CONTACT PERSON: Ann Crilly, Senior Library Assistant in charge

DESCRIPTION:
Small but attractive library in a historic building with a collection of just over 6,000 volumes in a wide range of subject areas.

SERVICES:
Finding aids; information of local interest; parking.

SEE ALSO: SOUTH EASTERN EDUCATION AND LIBRARY BOARD, Ballynahinch

CAVAN COUNTY COUNCIL BRANCH
LIBRARIES HEADQUARTERS
Farnham Street
CAVAN TOWN, COUNTY CAVAN

NOTE: The Cavan County Council operates twelve libraries throughout the county, only two of which, the Cavan Town Branch Library and the Bailieboro Branch Library, operate full-time. The part-time libraries are listed here, while separate listings are provided for the Cavan Town Branch Library and the Bailieboro Branch Library. Telephone numbers are not available for the part-time libraries. Visitors are welcome, but borrowing privileges limited.

ARVA LIBRARY: Health Centre, Arva, Co. Cavan

HOURS:
MON 3:00 pm–5:00 pm, 7:00 pm–9:00 pm;
WED, SAT: 7:00 pm–9:00 pm;
FRI: 3:00 pm–5:00 pm

BALLINAGH LIBRARY: Community Centre,
Ballinagh, Co. Cavan

HOURS:
MON, TH: 3:00 pm–5:00 pm, 7:30 pm–9:00 pm

BALLYCONNELL LIBRARY: Church Street,
Ballyconnell, Co. Cavan

HOURS:
WED, FR: 3:00 pm–6:00 pm, 7:00 pm–9:00 pm;
TH: 3:00 pm–6:00 pm;
SAT: 11:00 am– 2:00 pm

BALLYJAMESDUFF LIBRARY: Health Centre,
Percy French Park, Ballyjamesduff, Co. Cavan

HOURS:
MON, FRI: 3:00 pm–5:30 pm;
WED: 3:00 pm–5:00 pm, 7:00 pm–8:30 pm

BELTURBET LIBRARY: Town Hall, Belturbet,
Co. Cavan

HOURS:
MON, FRI: 3:00 pm–5:30 pm, 7:00 pm–8:30 pm;
WED: 3:00 pm–5:00 pm

COOTEHILL LIBRARY, Courthouse, Cootehill,
Co. Cavan

HOURS:
TUE: 6:30 pm–9:30 pm;
SAT: 9:30 am–1:00 pm

KILLESHANDRA LIBRARY, Community
Centre, Killeshandra, Co. Cavan

HOURS:
MON, FR: 3:00 pm–5:00 pm;
WED: 7:00 pm–8:00 pm

KILNALECK LIBRARY: Community Centre,
Kilnaleck, Co. Cavan

HOURS:
TUE: 3:00 pm–5:00 pm;
TH: 7:00 pm–8:30 pm

KINGSCOURT LIBRARY, St. Mary's Hall,
Kingscourt, Co. Cavan

HOURS:
MON, WED: 3:00 pm–5:00 pm;

TH: 6:30 pm–8:00 pm;
FRI. 3:00 pm–5:00 pm, 6:30 pm–8:00 pm

VIRGINIA LIBRARY:
Health Centre, Bailieboro Rd
VIRGINIA, CO. CAVAN

HOURS:
MON, FRI: 3:00 pm–5:00 pm, 7:00 pm–8:00 pm;
WED: 3:00 pm–5:00 pm;
SAT: 11:00 am–1:00 pm

CAVAN COUNTY MUSEUM
SEE UNDER BALLYJAMESDUFF

CAVAN GENEALOGICAL RESEARCH CENTRE
SEE COUNTY CAVAN GENEALOGICAL RESEARCH CENTRE, Cavan

CAVAN TOWN BRANCH LIBRARY
Farnham Street
CAVAN, COUNTY CAVAN

TELEPHONE: 049–31799; FAX: 049–31384

HOURS:
MON, TH: 11:00 am–1:00 pm, 2:00 pm–5:00 pm, 6:00 pm–8:30 pm;
TUE, WED: 11:00 am–5:00 pm;
FRI: 11:00 am–1:00 pm, 2:00 pm–5:00 pm;
CHILDREN'S LIBRARY OPEN MON–FRI: 2:00 pm–5:00 pm.

ACCESS:
Visitors welcome, but borrowing privileges limited.
Handicapped accessible.

CONTACT PERSON: Mrs. Josephine Brady, County
Librarian

DESCRIPTION:
Flagship library of the County Cavan library system.
Strong local history collection.

SPECIAL COLLECTIONS:
Local history collection exceeds 3,500 volumes,
including many 18th and 19th-century books on Cavan
Town and County Cavan; strong holdings of maps,

including 1835 Ordnance Survey for Cavan, Cavan-Leitrim Railway, and the South Western Section of Farnham Estate; important holdings of a social and genealogical concern, including Cavan Assizes, 1807-1851, which record individuals charged with crimes and the verdicts rendered; 18th and 19th-century legal documents, such as leases, rentals and wills for County Cavan; registers, account and fee books and inspectors reports from Bailieboro Model School, 1860s-1900s; minute books for the Board of Guardian (1839-1921) and the Rural District Council (1899-1925); diaries, including the diary of Randal McCollum, Presbyterian minister, Shercock, Co. Cavan, describing social conditions in Cavan, 1861-1871; photographs and postcards; and the correspondence and papers of various local personages. There is also an extensive microfilm and photocopy collection of materials relating to County Cavan, especially rich in family history sources; newspaper holdings and directories.

SERVICES:
Photocopying, with some restrictions on material; microfilm reader/printer; nearby car parks and limited on-street parking.

COUNTY CAVAN GENEALOGICAL RESEARCH CENTRE
Cana House, Farnham Street
CAVAN, COUNTY CAVAN

TELEPHONE: 049–61094; FAX: 049–31494

HOURS:
MAY–SEPTEMBER:
MON–FRI: 9:30 am–4:30 pm;
SAT: By appointment;
OCTOBER–APRIL:
MON–TH. 9:30 am–4:30 pm;
FRI: 9:30 am–1:00 pm

ACCESS:
Private and publicly-funded genealogical research centre open to the public. Not handicapped accessible. There is no admission fee, but fees are charged for research services. A schedule of fees is available from the centre on request. Fees vary depending on service required and time involved. Fees currently range between £10 and £150.

C

CONTACT PERSON: Mrs. Mary Sullivan, Manager

DESCRIPTION:
County Cavan Genealogical Research Centre is one of seven centres in the nine counties of Ulster that participate in the Irish Genealogical Project (IGP). This project aims to create a comprehensive database of all genealogical sources that are known to exist, including church records of all denominations, civil records, land valuations, census records, gravestone inscriptions and various other local sources. The Cavan Centre offers a genealogical research service for County Cavan. The Centre is computerizing the standard sources, i.e, pre-1900 church registers, civil records from 1864, tithe applotment books (1823-1837), Griffith's Valuation (1856-1857), the 1901 Census, the surviving returns from the 1821 Census for 16 County Cavan parishes, and graveyard inscriptions (20 completed). In addition, the Centre is compiling data from various other sources, including Hearth Money Rolls, Poll Book for County Cavan, Flax Growers list, Registry of Freeholders, Relief Commission Papers, Parish histories, and some school rolls.

SERVICES:
In addition to research services, the Centre offers for sale various parish histories and other books relating to County Cavan. It sells the current journal of the local historical society, *Breiffne*, plus back issues. It also sells miscellaneous items of a genealogical interest, such as family crests and family tree books.

SEE ALSO:
ARMAGH ANCESTRY, Armagh; ULSTER HISTORICAL FOUNDATION, Belfast; THE GENEALOGY CENTRE, Derry; HERITAGE WORLD, Dungannon; MONAGHAN ANCESTRY, Monaghan; and DONEGAL ANCESTRY, Ramelton. Also: GENERAL REGISTER OFFICE, Belfast; and PUBLIC RECORD OFFICE OF NORTHERN IRELAND, Belfast.

MONAGHAN COUNTY LIBRARY
The Diamond
CLONES, COUNTY MONAGHAN

TELEPHONE: 047–51143

HOURS:
MON: 2:00 pm–5:00 pm, 6:00 pm–8:00 pm;
WED, TH, FRI: 2:00 pm–5:00 pm

ACCESS:
Visitors welcome, but identification required.
Borrowing privileges for visitors are available but
limited. Consult with Librarian.

CONTACT PERSON: Joe McElvaney, County Librarian

DESCRIPTION:
Headquarters library for the Monaghan County Library
system that includes four branch libraries: Ballybay,
Carrickmacross, Castleblayney, and Monaghan.

SPECIAL COLLECTIONS:
Good local history collection, supported by a general
collection of Irish interest.

CLONMANY BRANCH LIBRARY
SEE DONEGAL COUNTY LIBRARY ADMINISTRATIVE CENTRE,
Letterkenny

CLOUGHMILLS BRANCH LIBRARY
Cloughmills PS, Main Street
CLOGHMILLS, BT44 9LG

TELEPHONE: 012656–38537

HOURS:
TUE, TH: 2:00 pm–5:00 pm, 5:30 pm–8:00 pm;
FRI: 2:00 pm–5:00 pm;
SAT: 10:00 am–1:00 pm

ACCESS:
Visitors welcome, but identification required. Borrowing
privileges for visitors may be restricted. Consult with
Librarian.

CONTACT PERSON: Mrs. A.M. Dickson, Senior Library
Assistant in charge

SEE ALSO: NORTH EASTERN EDUCATION AND LIBRARY
BOARD, Ballymena

CLOUGHFERN BRANCH LIBRARY
SEE UNDER Newtownabbey

COALISLAND BRANCH LIBRARY
The Cornhill
COALISLAND, BT71 4LT

TELEPHONE: 01868–740569

HOURS:
MON, TUE, FRI: 10:00 am–6:00 pm;
TH: 10:00 am–8:00 pm;
SAT: 10:00 am–5:00 pm

ACCESS:
Visitors welcome, but identification required. Borrowing privileges for visitors may be restricted. Consult with Librarian.

CONTACT PERSON: Mrs. G. Hamilton

SEE ALSO: SOUTHERN EDUCATION AND LIBRARY BOARD, Armagh

COOTEHILL BRANCH LIBRARY
SEE CAVAN COUNTY COUNCIL BRANCH LIBRARIES, Cavan

CORNMILL HERITAGE CENTRE
Lineside
COALISLAND, CO. TYRONE

TELEPHONE: 01868–748532; FAX: 01868–748695

HOURS:
JUNE–SEPTEMBER:
MON–FRI: 10:00 am–8:00 pm;
SAT: 11:00 am–6:00 pm;
SUN: 2:00 pm–6:00 pm;
OCTOBER–MAY:
MON–FRI: 10:00 am–6:00 pm

ACCESS:
Open to the public. Admission charged. Current fees: Adults = £1.50; Child = £0.80; Students and Seniors = £1.20; special family and group rates available. Handicapped accessible.

CONTACT PERSON: Project Manager

DESCRIPTION:
Located in the heart of Ulster, close to the southwestern shore of Lough Neagh, the original corn mill opened in

1907 and closed in 1978. The cornmill was renovated beginning in 1990 as a heritage centre to interpret four centuries of Coalisland's industrial past through exhibitions featuring paintings, photographs, reconstructions, industrial artefacts and murals. It is especially strong in telling the story of the Industrial Revolution in Ireland. While it maintains no library or archive, it does offer a good introduction to Ireland's industrial past.

SERVICES:
Exhibitions; retail outlet stocking local craft; research unit; free parking.

IRISH ROOM
County Hall, Castlerock Road
COLERAINE, BT1 3HP

TELEPHONE: 01265–51026; FAX: 01265–51247

HOURS:
MON–FRI: 1:30 pm–4:30 pm

ACCESS:
Visitors welcome, but identification required. Borrowing privileges for visitors may be restricted. Consult with Librarian. Almost the entire collection is catalogued on cards, with only about 1% catalogued in machine readable form. Handicapped accessible.

CONTACT PERSON: Mrs. L. Buick, Local Studies Librarian

DESCRIPTION:
The Irish Room houses a collection of more than 13,000 volumes, about 100 journals, and modest collections of maps, photographs and microforms focusing on the local history of the area covered by the NEELB. Though the intent of the collection is to be comprehensive, this collection has remained static since 1973 except for donations, local newspapers and some journal titles.

SPECIAL COLLECTIONS:
Hugh Thomson Collection, containing books illustrated by this artist, who was born in Coleraine in 1860 and died in 1920.

SERVICES:
Photocopying, brochures, ample free parking at County Hall complex.

SEE ALSO: NORTH EASTERN EDUCATION AND LIBRARY BOARD, Ballymena

COLERAINE BRANCH LIBRARY
Queen Street
COLERAINE, BT52 1BE

TELEPHONE: 01265–42561

HOURS:
MON, TUE, FRI: 10:00 am–8:00 pm;
WED, TH: 10:00 am–5:30 pm;
SAT: 10:00 am–5:00 pm

ACCESS:
Visitors welcome, but identification required. Borrowing privileges for visitors may be restricted. Consult with Librarian.

CONTACT PERSON: Mr. B. Porter, District Librarian in charge

SEE ALSO: NORTH EASTERN EDUCATION AND LIBRARY BOARD, Ballymena

UNIVERSITY OF ULSTER AT COLERAINE
COLERAINE, BT52 1SA

TELEPHONE: 01265–44141; FAX: 01265–40928

HOURS:
TERM: MON–FR: 9:00 am–10:00 pm;
SAT: 10:00 am–5:00 pm;
VACATION: MON–TH: 9:00 am–5:00 pm;
FRI: 9:00 am–4:00 pm

ACCESS:
Publicly-funded University library open to the public for reference purposes. Visitors welcome, but identification required. Borrowing privileges may be restricted. Consult with Librarian. Collection catalogued in machine readable form. Handicapped accessible.

CONTACT PERSON: Ms. Nicky-Sinead Gardner, Director of Educational Services

DESCRIPTION:
Main campus of the four-campus University of Ulster system, Coleraine maintains two libraries: the Central Buildings Library which houses materials for

Humanities, Science and Technology, and the South
Building Library, which contains materials for
Education, Social and Health Sciences, Business and
Management and Informatics. The total number of
volumes for the four-campus system exceeds 600,000.

SPECIAL COLLECTIONS:
Special Collections is located in the Central Buildings
Library. It boasts several impressive collections,
including the Henry Davis Collection of early and rare
printed books featuring 80 incunabula, i.e., books
printed before 1501; the Irish Collection, recently
enhanced by the additions of the collection of Irish
folklorist Henry Morris, and the library and archive of
writer Francis Stuart; the Headlam-Morley Collection on
World War I; the library of Belfast poet John Hewitt and
the papers of playwright George Shiels.

SERVICES:
Photocopying; database searching; microfilm/fiche/
reader/printer; brochures; finding aids; free parking by
prior arrangement.

SEE ALSO:
UNIVERSITY OF ULSTER AT BELFAST, Belfast; UNIVERSITY
OF ULSTER, MAGEE COLLEGE, Derry; and UNIVERSITY OF
ULSTER AT JORDANSTOWN, Jordanstown

COOKSTOWN BRANCH LIBRARY
Burn Road
COOKSTOWN, BT80 8DJ

TELEPHONE: 016487–63702

HOURS:
MON, WED, FRI: 9:30 am–5:30 pm;
TUE, TH: 9:30 am–8:00 pm;
SAT: 9:30 am–5:00 pm

ACCESS:
Visitors welcome, but identification required. Borrowing
privileges for visitors may be restricted. Consult with
Librarian.

CONTACT PERSON: Mrs. Y. Baxter

SEE ALSO: SOUTHERN EDUCATION AND LIBRARY BOARD,
Armagh

C

LOUGHRY COLLEGE
THE FOOD CENTRE
COOKSTOWN, BT80 9AA

TELEPHONE: 016487–68111, EXT. 214; FAX: 016487–61043
E-MAIL: loughry.food.centre.dani@nics.gov.uk
WEB SITE: http://www.nics.gov.uk/dani/loughry/

HOURS:
TERM: MON–TH: 9:30 am–9:30 pm;
FRI: 9:30 am–5:00 pm;
VACATION: MON–WED: 9:30 am–5:00 pm
TH: 9:30 am–9.00 pm

ACCESS:
Publicly-funded food technology college open to the
public for reference purposes. Visitors welcome, but
please telephone or write in advance. Borrowing
privileges may be restricted. Consult with Librarian.
Card catalogue. Limited handicapped access.

CONTACT PERSON: Ms. Jacki Sleator, Librarian

DESCRIPTION:
Small academic library of some 10,000 books to serve
the needs of faculty and students in the areas of food
technology and communications.

SERVICES:
Photocopying; free parking; accessions lists.

COOTEHILL BRANCH LIBRARY
SEE CAVAN COUNTY COUNCIL BRANCH LIBRARIES, Cavan

BROWNLOW BRANCH LIBRARY
Brownlow Road, Legahory
CRAIGAVON, BT65 5DP

TELEPHONE: 01762–341946

HOURS:
MON, WED: 10:00 am–5:30 pm;
TUE, TH: 10:00 am–8:00 pm;
FRI, SAT: 10:00 am–5:00 pm

ACCESS:
Visitors welcome, but identification required. Borrowing
privileges for visitors may be restricted. Consult with
Librarian.

CONTACT PERSON: Mr. M. McDonagh, Branch Librarian

SEE ALSO: SOUTHERN EDUCATION AND LIBRARY BOARD,
Armagh

CRAIGAVON DIVISIONAL LIBRARY
HEADQUARTERS
SEE UNDER Portadown

MOIRA LIBRARY
Backwood Road
MOIRA, CRAIGAVON, BT67 OLJ

TELEPHONE: 01846–619330

HOURS:
MON, SAT: 10:00 am–1:00 pm;
TUE, TH: 2:00 pm–8:00 pm;
FR: 2:00 pm–5:00 pm

ACCESS:
Visitors welcome, but identification required. Borrowing
privileges for visitors may be restricted. Consult with
Librarian.

CONTACT PERSON: Mrs. Ann Bell, Branch Librarian

SEE ALSO: SOUTH EASTERN EDUCATION AND LIBRARY BOARD,
Ballynahinch

CROSSMAGLEN BRANCH LIBRARY
The Square
CROSSMAGLEN, BT35 9AA

TELEPHONE: 01693–861951

HOURS:
TUE, FRI: 10:00 am–1:00 pm, 2:00 pm–6:00 pm;
WED: 1:00 pm–6:00 pm;
SAT. 10:00 am–4:30 pm

ACCESS:
Visitors welcome, but identification required. Borrowing
privileges for visitors may be restricted. Consult with
Librarian.

CONTACT PERSON: Mrs. R. McDonnell

SEE ALSO: SOUTHERN EDUCATION AND LIBRARY BOARD,
Armagh

CRUMLIN BRANCH LIBRARY
Orchard Road
CRUMLIN, BT29 4SD

TELEPHONE: 01849–423066

HOURS:
TUE: 10:30 am–1:00 pm, 2:00 pm–5:30 pm;
WED, FRI: 2:00 pm–5:00 pm, 6:00 pm–8:00 pm;
SAT: 10:30 am–1:00 pm, 2:00 pm–5:00 pm

ACCESS:
Visitors welcome, but identification required. Borrowing privileges for visitors may be restricted. Consult with Librarian.

CONTACT PERSON: Miss S. Sullivan, Senior Library Assistant in charge

SEE ALSO: NORTH EASTERN EDUCATION AND LIBRARY BOARD, Ballymena

CULLYBACKEY BRANCH LIBRARY
153 Tobar Park
CULLYBACKEY, BT42 1NW

TELEPHONE: 01266–881878

HOURS:
TUE, FRI: 2:30 pm–5:00 pm, 5:30 pm–8:00 pm;
TH, SAT: 10:30 am–1:00 pm, 2:00 pm–5:00 pm

ACCESS:
Visitors welcome, but identification required. Borrowing privileges for visitors may be restricted. Consult with Librarian.

CONTACT PERSON: Mrs. M. Donaghy, Senior Library Assistant in charge

SEE ALSO: NORTH EASTERN EDUCATION AND LIBRARY BOARD, Ballymena

ULSTER FOLK AND TRANSPORT MUSEUM
CULTRA, HOLYWOOD, BT18 0EU

TELEPHONE: 01232–428428; FAX: 01232–428728

HOURS:
JULY–AUGUST: MON–SAT: 10:30 am–6:00 pm;

SUN: 12:00 pm–6:00 pm;
APRIL–JUNE, SEPTEMBER: MON–FRI: 9:30 am–5:00 pm;
SAT: 10:30 am–6:00 pm;
SUN: 12:00 pm–6:00 pm;
OCTOBER–MARCH: MON–FRI: 9:30 am–4:00 pm;
SAT–SUN: 12:30 pm–4:30 pm

ACCESS:
Museum is open to general public. Admission charged.
Current fees: Adult = £3.30; Child = £2.20; group,
family, student, and senior rates available. Mostly
handicapped accessible. For access to the library and
archives, please make appointment.

CONTACT PERSON: Roger Dixon, Librarian

DESCRIPTION:
Extensive grounds comprising 177 acres devoted to
preserving the way things were in the north of Ireland,
especially around the turn of the century. Reconstructed
farms, houses, workshops, mills, schools, churches and
other facilities take visitors back in time. Traditional
crafts and occupations are demonstrated and taught. The
transport museums exhibit various modes of
transportation from old railroad engines and cars to the
modern DeLorean automobile, manufactured in Belfast.
The Irish Railway Collection is one of the newest and
most interesting exhibits. Museum also houses a library
and archive.

SPECIAL COLLECTIONS:
Library and archive collections support the various
interests of the museum, especially folk life, social
history and transport. The book collection of some
20,000 volumes is available for reference purposes only.
The archive boasts an extensive collection of
photographs from the late nineteenth century to the
present. The largest photograph collection is the 70,000-
item archive of Harland and Wolff Limited, which
records the shipbuilding activity of this company from
1895 to the mid-1980s. Harland and Wolff built the
Titanic. The Museum also archives an extensive and
comprehensive collection of sound recordings
documenting stories, language, music, customs, beliefs
and traditions. Recent additions include the BBC (NI)
archive and the tape-recorded survey of Hiberno-English
compiled throughout Ireland. The Museum also
maintains an Ulster Dialect Archive, and is compiling an
Ulster Dialect Dictionary onto a computer database.

PUBLICATIONS:
The Museum publishes a wide range of material,
including the journal *Ulster Folklife*, exhibition
catalogues, educational study packs and worksheets for
schools.

SERVICES:
Library offers reference assistance, photocopying,
microfilm reader/printer; photographic reproductions,
database searching. Museum offers restaurants and
shops, special events, indoor exhibitions, ample parking.

SEE ALSO:
ARMAGH COUNTY MUSEUM, Armagh; CAVAN COUNTY
MUSEUM, Ballyjamesduff; NORTH DOWN HERITAGE
CENTRE, Bangor; ULSTER MUSEUM, Belfast; TOWER
MUSEUM, Derry; DOWN COUNTY MUSEUM; Downpatrick;
ENNISKILLEN CASTLE, Enniskillen; DONEGAL COUNTY
MUSEUM, Letterkenny; IRISH LINEN CENTRE AND LISBURN
MUSEUM, Lisburn; MONAGHAN COUNTY MUSEUM,
Monaghan; and ULSTER-AMERICAN FOLK PARK, Omagh.

CUSHENDALL BRANCH LIBRARY
Mill Street
CUSHENDALL, BT44 0RR

TELEPHONE: 012667–71297

HOURS:
TUE, FRI: 2:30 pm–5:00 pm, 5:30 pm–8:00 pm;
TH, SAT: 10:30 am–1:00 pm, 2:00 pm–5:00 pm

ACCESS:
Visitors welcome, but identification required. Borrowing
privileges for visitors may be restricted. Consult with
Librarian.

CONTACT PERSON: Mrs. A. Blaney, Senior Library
Assistant in charge

SEE ALSO: NORTH EASTERN EDUCATION AND LIBRARY
BOARD, Ballymena

NOTE: Some of the following institutions use the designation Derry, others Londonderry. For consistency, all institutions are listed under Derry, the name adopted by the City Council. The county, however, is designated as Derry or Londonderry according to institutional preference, as listings are arranged by city or town and not by county.

CENTRAL LIBRARY
35 Foyle Street
DERRY, BT48 6AL

TELEPHONE: 01504–266888; FAX: 01504–269084
E–MAIL: trishaw@online.rednet.co.uk

HOURS:
MON, TH: 9:15 am–8:00 pm;
TUE, WED, FRI: 9:15 am–5:30 pm;
SAT. 9:15 am–5:00 pm

ACCESS:
Visitors welcome, but identification required. Borrowing privileges for visitors may be restricted. Consult with librarian. Handicapped accessible. General stacks open, but stacks in special collections closed. Entire collection catalogued in machine readable form.

CONTACT PERSON: Mrs. Patricia. Ward, Senior Librarian; Mrs. Maura Craig, Senior Librarian in charge of local history collection; Anne Peoples, Divisional Librarian

DESCRIPTION:
Opened in 1990, this handsome facility is the main branch library for Derry, located just outside the city walls, with an important Irish and local studies department. The collection totals more than 72,000 volumes, plus some 3,000 recordings.

SPECIAL COLLECTIONS:
Irish and local studies collections include some 15,000 volumes, 2,500 photographs and 2,000 maps with special emphasis on the west of Co. Londonderry, including Limavady and Dungiven. Also local newspapers on microfilm dating back to 1829, ordnance

survey maps, and local history files. Central Library also houses the business collection for WELB.

SERVICES:
Photocopying and microfilm printout available. Linked via computer to the emigration database of the Ulster-American Folk Park, Omagh. City car park nearby.

SEE ALSO: WESTERN EDUCATION AND LIBRARY BOARD, Omagh

CREGGAN BRANCH LIBRARY
Central Drive, Creggan Estate
DERRY, BT48 9QH

TELEPHONE: 01504–266168

HOURS:
MON: 1:00 pm–7:30 pm;
TUE, FRI: 10:00 am–5:30 pm;
WED: 10:00 am–7:30 pm;
SAT: 9:00 am–1:00 pm

ACCESS:
Visitors welcome, but identification required. Borrowing privileges for visitors may be restricted. Consult with Librarian.

CONTACT PERSON: Mr. J. Campbell

SEE ALSO: WESTERN EDUCATION AND LIBRARY BOARD, Omagh

THE GENEALOGY CENTRE
Pump Street
DERRY, BT48 6HL

TELEPHONE: 01504–261967; FAX: 01504–360921

HOURS:
MON–FRI: 9:00 am–5:00 pm

ACCESS:
Open to the public. Research services provided for a modest fee. No direct access to database. Application may be made by telephone, letter or in person.

Handicapped accessible.

CONTACT PERSON: Brian Mitchell, Director

DESCRIPTION:
Sponsored by the Inner City Trust, The Genealogy
Centre is one of seven designated centres in the nine
counties of Ulster that participate in the Irish
Genealogical Project (IGP). This project aims to create a
comprehensive database of all genealogical sources that
are known to exist, including church records of all
denominations, civil records, land valuations, census
records, gravestone inscriptions and various other local
sources. The Genealogy Centre offers a genealogical
research service for County Londonderry and Inishowen
Peninsula, County Donegal. The database now exceeds
one million entries. There is an initial search fee of £20.

SPECIAL COLLECTIONS:
The Centre collects copies of birth, marriage, and death
certificates, church registers, gravestone inscriptions,
Griffith's valuation, tithe books and the 1901 census for
County Londonderry to input them on the database. The
reference collection also includes emigration books and
some passenger lists.

SERVICES:
Database searching; consultation; brochures; shop; car
parks nearby.

PUBLICATIONS:
Centre publishes books of genealogical or local history
interest; e.g., *Irish Passenger Lists, 1803-1806; A New
Genealogical Atlas of Ireland*; and *The Making of
Derry: An Economic History*.

SEE ALSO:
ARMAGH ANCESTRY, Armagh; ULSTER HISTORICAL
FOUNDATION, Belfast; CAVAN GENEALOGICAL RESEARCH
CENTRE, Cavan; HERITAGE WORLD, Dungannon;
MONAGHAN ANCESTRY, Monaghan; and DONEGAL
ANCESTRY, Ramelton. ALSO: GENERAL REGISTER OFFICE,
Belfast; and the PUBLIC RECORD OFFICE OF NORTHERN
IRELAND, Belfast.

HERITAGE AND MUSEUM SERVICE
Harbour Museum. Harbour Square
DERRY, BT48 6AF

TELEPHONE: 01504–377331; FAX: 01504–377317

HOURS:
MON–FRI: 9:00 am–1:00 pm, 2:00 pm–5:00 pm

ACCESS:
Publicly-funded (Derry City Council) museum and
library/archive open to visitors at no charge. Informal
application procedures. Some stacks closed to public.
Consult Programme Organizer. No handicapped access.
Library and archive services are still in embryonic stage.

CONTACT PERSON: Mr. Brian Lacy, Programme Organizer.

DESCRIPTION:
Museum is located in an 1880 building converted for
museum/archive in 1993. Collects material documenting
the local history of Derry City and surrounding region.
Of special interest is the Derry City Council archive
detailing the growth and development of the city from
the late seventeenth century onwards. Exhibits focus on
Derry's maritime tradition.

SERVICES:
Exhibitions; brochures; city car park nearby.

HERITAGE LIBRARY
SEE THE GENEALOGY CENTRE, Derry

THE INNER CITY TRUST
SEE THE GENEALOGY CENTRE, Derry

MAGEE COLLEGE
SEE UNIVERSITY OF ULSTER, MAGEE COLLEGE, Derry

MULTI-DISCIPLINARY EDUCATION CENTRE LIBRARY
Altnagelvin Area Hospital, Glenshane Road
DERRY, BT47 1JB

TELEPHONE: 01504–45171, EXT. 3725; FAX: 01504–49334

HOURS:
SEPTEMBER–JUNE: MON, FRI: 9:00 am–5:00 pm;
TUE–TH: 9:00 am–9:30 pm

ACCESS:
Publicly-funded library for health service professionals.
Visitors welcome to use library for reference purposes
but may not borrow material. Appointment and
identification required. Reference letter required for
long-term use. Contact Librarian. Collection is
catalogued in machine readable form. Handicapped
accessibility limited.

CONTACT PERSON: Mr. F. A. O'Deorain, Library Manager.

DESCRIPTION:
The library, established in 1983, contains some 9,000
books and 120 periodical titles designed to support the
post-graduate education and clinical practice of all
professional groups in the National Health Service in the
Western Health & Social Services Board area.
Collection focuses on nursing, medicine, paramedical,
social work and health service management.

SERVICES:
Photocopying; printed guides; database searching; free
parking.

NORTH WEST DIVISIONAL LIBRARY
35 Foyle Street
DERRY, BT48 6AL

TELEPHONE: 01504–266888

HOURS:
MON–FRI: 9:00 am–5:00 pm

ACCESS:
By appointment

CONTACT PERSON: Ms. Anne Peoples, Divisional
Librarian

DESCRIPTION:
Oversees and coordinates operations of the branch
libraries in the North West area of the Western

Education and Library Board, i.e., Derry Central, Derry Creggan, Derry Shantallow, Derry Waterside, Dungiven, Limavady, and Strathfoyle.

SEE ALSO: WESTERN EDUCATION AND LIBRARY BOARD, Omagh

NORTH WEST INSTITUTE OF FURTHER AND HIGHER EDUCATION
Strand Road
DERRY, BT48 7BY

TELEPHONE: 01504–266711; FAX: 01504–267054;
E-MAIL: memc@nwifhe.demon.co.uk

HOURS:
TERM: MON–TH: 9:00 am–9:00 pm;
FRI: 9:00 am–4:30 pm;
VACATION: MON–TH: 9:00 am–1:00 pm, 2:00 pm–5:00 pm;
FRI: 9:00 am–1:00 pm, 2:00 pm–4:30 pm

ACCESS:
Academic library. Visitors welcome, but identification required. Advance notification preferred. Collection is classified by Dewey and is catalogued in machine readable form. Handicapped accessible.

CONTACT PERSON: Mrs. Madeleine Coyle, Librarian

DESCRIPTION:
Collection is designed to support the teaching and training curriculum of the Institute, including the subject areas of Arts and General Studies, Business and Management Studies, Construction and Allied Services, Engineering, Mathematics, Science, Computing, Caring, Secretarial Studies and Social Education.

SPECIAL COLLECTIONS:
Small Irish collection.

SERVICES:
Photocopying; printed guide; public car park nearby.

SHANTALLOW BRANCH LIBRARY
92 Racecourse Road
DERRY, BT48 8DA

TELEPHONE: 01504–762540

HOURS:
MON, FRI: 10:00 am–5:30 pm,
TUE, TH: 10:00 am–7:30 pm;
SAT: 9:15 am–1:00 pm

ACCESS:
Visitors welcome, but identification required. Borrowing privileges for visitors may be restricted. Consult with Librarian.

CONTACT PERSON: Ms. J. Cusac

SEE ALSO: WESTERN EDUCATION AND LIBRARY BOARD, Omagh

TOWER MUSEUM
Union Hall Place
DERRY, BT48 6LU

TELEPHONE: 01504–372411

HOURS:
TUE–SAT: 10:00 am–5:00 pm;
Also open 2.00 pm–5:00 pm on Sundays in July and August and on all Bank Holiday Mondays throughout the year

ACCESS:
Open to general public for admission fee. Current fees:
Adult = £3.00; Child = £1.00; Preschoolers and seniors = free; group and family rates available.

CONTACT PERSON: Mr. Brian Lacy, Director

DESCRIPTION:
Operated by the Derry City Council Heritage and Museum Service, the Tower Museum maintains a permanent exhibition outlining the history and development of the ancient city of Derry from prehistoric times to the present. This exhibit features a wide variety of interesting media and theatrical presentations plus historical and archaeological artefacts to convey the story of Derry. The Heritage and Museum Service also operates the Foyle Valley Railway Centre, the Amelia Earhart College, and the HARBOUR MUSEUM.

SERVICES:
Special exhibitions; souvenir shop; nearby public car park.

SEE ALSO:
ARMAGH COUNTY MUSEUM, Armagh; CAVAN COUNTY
MUSEUM, Ballyjamesduff; NORTH DOWN HERITAGE CENTRE,
Bangor; ULSTER MUSEUM, Belfast; ULSTER FOLK AND
TRANSPORT MUSEUM, Cultra; DOWN COUNTY MUSEUM;
Downpatrick; ENNISKILLEN CASTLE, Enniskillen;
DONEGAL COUNTY MUSEUM, Letterkenny; IRISH LINEN
CENTRE AND LISBURN MUSEUM, Lisburn; MONAGHAN
COUNTY MUSEUM, Monaghan; and ULSTER-AMERICAN FOLK
PARK, Omagh.

UNIVERSITY OF ULSTER
Magee College, Northland Road
DERRY, BT48 7JL

TELEPHONE: 01504–375240; FAX: 01504–375626
E-MAIL: pd.teskey@ulst.ac.uk

HOURS:
TERM: MON–FRI: 9:00 am–9:00 pm;
SAT: 9:00 am–5:00 pm;
VACATION: MON–FRI: 9:00 am–5:00 pm

ACCESS:
A publicly-funded university, Magee is the western
branch of the four-campus University of Ulster system.
Visitors welcome, but borrowing and database searching
privileges may be restricted. Consult with Librarian.
Application for access to Special Collections is
preferred. About three-fourths of the collection is
catalogued in machine readable form, the balance on
cards. Handicapped accessible.

CONTACT PERSON: Patrick Teskey, Sub-Librarian

DESCRIPTION:
Magee was founded in 1865 to prepare entrants for the
Presbyterian ministry, and in 1984 Magee University
College became part of the University of Ulster. The new
library, opened in 1990, houses some 100,000 volumes
and 600 current periodicals. The collection supports the
academic mission of Magee, with strong holdings on
Irish history and politics.

SPECIAL COLLECTIONS:
The Irish Collection includes some 6,000 books and 900

pamphlets. There is also a good eighteenth-century printing collection, with special emphasis on Irish printing. Other interests: the Spalding Collection on Eastern Civilizations; a small collection (51 manuscripts) on Irish Presbyterianism: Stewart, Duchal and Witherow manuscript collections, and a collection of some 3,000 photographic negatives of local interest.

SERVICES:
Photocopying; database searching; brochures; ample parking.

SEE ALSO:
UNIVERSITY OF ULSTER AT BELFAST, Belfast; UNIVERSITY OF ULSTER, Coleraine; and UNIVERSITY OF ULSTER AT JORDANSTOWN, Jordanstown

WATERSIDE BRANCH LIBRARY
137 Spencer Road
DERRY, BT47 1AQ

TELEPHONE: 01504–42963

HOURS:
MON: 10:00 am–7:30 pm;
TUE–TH: 10:00 am–5:30 pm; 10:00 am–7:30 pm;
SAT: 9:15 am–1:00 pm

ACCESS:
Visitors welcome, but identification required. Borrowing privileges for visitors may be restricted. Consult with Librarian. About 80% of collection catalogued in machine readable form. Not handicapped accessible.

CONTACT PERSON: Mrs. J. Austin, Branch Librarian; Ms. Anne Peoples, Divisional Librarian

DESCRIPTION:
Opened in 1966 in the Waterside area of Derry, the library houses some 28,000 volumes of a general interest.

SEE ALSO: WESTERN EDUCATION AND LIBRARY BOARD, Omagh

DONAGHADEE BRANCH LIBRARY
5 Killaughey Road
DONAGHADEE, BT21 0BL

TELEPHONE: 01247–882507

HOURS:
MON–WED: 10:00 am–8:00 pm;
FRI: 10:00 am–5:00 pm;
SAT: 10:00 am–1:00 pm, 2:00 pm–5:00 pm

ACCESS:
Visitors welcome, but identification required. Borrowing privileges for visitors may be restricted. Consult with Librarian.

CONTACT PERSON: Mrs. Norma Millar, Branch Librarian

SEE ALSO: SOUTH EASTERN EDUCATION AND LIBRARY BOARD, Ballynahinch

DONEGAL BRANCH LIBRARY
SEE DONEGAL COUNTY LIBRARY ADMINISTRATIVE CENTRE, Letterkenny

DOWN COUNTY MUSEUM
The Mall
DOWNPATRICK, BT30 6AH

TELEPHONE: 01396–615218; FAX: 01396–61550

HOURS:
JUNE–AUGUST: TUE–FRI: 11:00 am–5:00 pm;
SAT: 2:00 pm–5:00 pm;
SUN: 2:00 pm–5:00 pm;
MON: 11:00 am–5:00 PM
SEPTEMBER–MAY: Closed Sundays and Mondays.

ACCESS:
The museum is open to the public, free of charge. Advance notice preferred to gain access to collections or meet with staff. Limited handicapped accessibility.

CONTACT PERSON: Dr. Brian. S. Turner; Director; Lesley Simpson, Keeper of Collection; Linda McKenna, Community Education Officer

D

DESCRIPTION:
This is a community history museum located near Down
Cathedral and St. Patrick's Grave. It occupies the
restored buildings of the old Down County Gaol, built
between 1789 and 1796. The museum features
permanent and changing exhibitions on County Down
history, archaeology and art, and exhibitions on St.
Patrick and the early Christian church.

SPECIAL COLLECTIONS:
Collection covers wide range of materials documenting
the history, life and culture of County Down from
prehistoric times to the present. The book collection
totals more than 6,500 volumes. There is also an
important photo archive.

SERVICES:
Temporary exhibitions; leaflets and handouts; education
and events programmes; free parking; shop; tea room.

SEE ALSO:
ARMAGH COUNTY MUSEUM, Armagh; NORTH DOWN
HERITAGE CENTRE, Bangor; ULSTER MUSEUM, Belfast;
ULSTER FOLK AND TRANSPORT MUSEUM, Cultra; TOWER
MUSEUM, Derry; DOWN COUNTY MUSEUM; Downpatrick;
ENNISKILLEN CASTLE, Enniskillen; IRISH LINEN CENTRE
AND LISBURN MUSEUM, Lisburn; and ULSTER-AMERICAN
FOLK PARK, Omagh.

DOWNPATRICK BRANCH LIBRARY
Market Street
DOWNPATRICK, BT30 6LZ

TELEPHONE: 01396–612895

HOURS:
MON, TUE, TH: 10:00 am–8:00 pm;
FRI: 10:00 am–5:00 pm;
SAT: 10:00 am–1:00 pm, 2:00 pm–5:00 pm

ACCESS:
Visitors welcome, but identification required. Borrowing
privileges for visitors may be restricted. Consult with
Librarian.

CONTACT PERSON: Miss Kathleen Smith, District
Librarian; Miss Ann Chestnutt, Branch Librarian

SEE ALSO: SOUTH EASTERN EDUCATION AND LIBRARY BOARD,
Ballynahinch

KILLYLEAGH BRANCH LIBRARY, Downpatrick
SEE UNDER Killyleagh

DRAPERSTOWN BRANCH LIBRARY
High Street
DRAPERSTOWN, BT45 7AD

TELEPHONE: 01648–28249

HOURS:
TUE, FRI: 2:00 pm–7:30 pm;
WED: 2:00 pm–5:00 pm;
SAT: 10:00 am–1:00 pm, 2:00 pm–5:00 pm

ACCESS:
Visitors welcome, but identification required. Borrowing
privileges for visitors may be restricted. Consult with
Librarian.

CONTACT PERSON: Mrs. E. Sewell, Senior Library
Assistant in charge

SPECIAL COLLECTIONS:
Draper's Company Reports and related source material
on the Plantation

SEE ALSO: NORTH EASTERN EDUCATION AND LIBRARY BOARD,
Ballymena

DROMORE BRANCH LIBRARY
Town Hall
DROMORE, BT25 1AW

TELEPHONE: 01846–692280

HOURS:
MON, TUE: 10:00 am–1:00 pm, 2:00 pm–5:30 pm;
WED, FRI: 10:00 am–1:00 pm, 2:00 pm–8:00 pm;
SAT: 10:00 am–1:00 pm, 2:00 pm–5:00 pm

ACCESS:
Visitors welcome, but identification required. Borrowing privileges for visitors may be restricted. Consult with Librarian.

CONTACT PERSON: Mrs. I. M. Given

SEE ALSO: SOUTHERN EDUCATION AND LIBRARY BOARD, Armagh

DUNGANNON BRANCH LIBRARY
Market Square
DUNGANNON, BT70 1JD

TELEPHONE: 01868–722952; FAX: 01868–753620

HOURS:
MON, WED, FRI: 9:30 am–5:30 pm;
TUE, TH: 9:30 am–8:00 pm;
SAT: 9:30 am–5:00 pm

ACCESS:
Visitors welcome, but identification required. Borrowing privileges for visitors may be restricted. Consult with Librarian.

CONTACT PERSON: Mrs. M. Montgomery

SEE ALSO: SOUTHERN EDUCATION AND LIBRARY BOARD, Armagh

DUNGANNON DIVISION LIBRARY
HEADQUARTERS
Market Square
DUNGANNON, BT70 1JD

TELEPHONE: 01868–722885; FAX: 01868–753620

HOURS:
MON–FRI: 9:00 am–5:00 pm

ACCESS:
By appointment

CONTACT PERSON: Mr. B. McGeown

SEE ALSO: SOUTHERN EDUCATION AND LIBRARY BOARD, Armagh

HERITAGE WORLD
26 Market Street
DUNGANNON, CO. TYRONE, BT70 1AB

TELEPHONE: 01868–724187; FAX: 01868–752141;
E–MAIL: irishwld@gpo.iol.ie

HOURS:
MON–TH: 9:00 am–5:00 pm;
FRI: 9:00 am–3:30 pm

ACCESS:
Private and publicly-funded genealogical service centre
open to the public. For schedule of fees, contact
Supervisor.

CONTACT PERSON: Feargal O'Donnell, Supervisor

DESCRIPTION:
One of seven centres covering the nine counties of
Ulster that participate in the Irish Genealogical Project
(IGP), an effort to create a comprehensive genealogical
database for all of Ireland from a wide variety of
sources, including church and state records, vital
records, tithe applotment books, Griffith's valuation, the
1901 census, and gravestone inscriptions. Heritage
World, formerly Irish World Family History, offers a
genealogical research service for County Tyrone and
County Fermanagh, but many of its records extend far
beyond these two counties. Its computerized records
include: pre-1900 church records of baptisms and
marriages for Tyrone and Fermanagh; civil records of
births and deaths (1864-1921) for Tyrone and
Fermanagh; civil marriage records (1845-1921) for
Tyrone and Fermanagh; 1901 census for Counties
Antrim, Armagh, Cavan, Derry, Donegal, Down,
Fermanagh, Monaghan and Tyrone; Griffith's Valuation
for all of Ireland (1848-1864); Tithe Applotment books
for Counties Antrim, Armagh, Derry, Down, Fermanagh
and Tyrone (1815-1837); gravestone inscriptions from
over 800 cemeteries for Counties Antrim, Armagh,
Derry, Down, Fermanagh and Tyrone; index to registry
of deeds for all of Ireland (1703-1904); index to wills for
all of Ireland (1858-1880); Irish directories (1751-1900);
flax growers list for all of Ireland (1796); transportation
records for all of Ireland (1839-1857) and index to Royal

Irish Constabulary records for all of Ireland (1816–1921). All told, the Centre boasts more than 7,000,000 records on computer.

SERVICES:
The Centre offers a small genealogical library for consultation, with special emphasis on Tyrone and Fermanagh. Locally produced crafts and genealogical aids are also available for purchase. The Centre also offers professional genealogical research services for a fee. Fees vary depending on service and time involved.

SEE ALSO:
ARMAGH ANCESTRY, Armagh; ULSTER HISTORICAL FOUNDATION, Belfast; CAVAN GENEALOGICAL RESEARCH CENTRE, Cavan; THE GENEALOGY CENTRE, Derry; MONAGHAN ANCESTRY, Monaghan; and DONEGAL ANCESTRY, Ramelton.

DUNGIVEN BRANCH LIBRARY
25 Main Street
DUNGIVEN, BT47 4LD

TELEPHONE: 015047–41475

HOURS:
MON: 2:00 pm–5:30 pm;
TUE, FRI: 10:00 am–1:00 pm, 2:00 pm–5:30 pm;
WED: 2:00 pm–7:00 pm;
SAT: 10:00 am–1:00 pm

ACCESS:
Visitors welcome, but identification required. Borrowing privileges for visitors may be restricted. Consult with Librarian.

CONTACT PERSON: Mrs. B. McCloskey

SEE ALSO: WESTERN EDUCATION AND LIBRARY BOARD, Omagh

DUNMURRY BRANCH LIBRARY
Upper Dunmurry Lane
DUNMURRY, BT17 0AA

TELEPHONE: 01232–623007

HOURS:
MON: 10:00 am–8:00 pm;
WED: 10:00 am–1:00 pm, 2:00 pm–8:00 pm;
FRI: 2:00 pm–5:00 pm;
SAT: 10:00 am–1:00 pm

ACCESS:
Visitors welcome, but identification required. Borrowing
privileges for visitors may be restricted. Consult with
Librarian.

CONTACT PERSON: Miss Josephine Quinn, Branch
Librarian

SEE ALSO: SOUTH EASTERN EDUCATION AND LIBRARY BOARD,
Ballynahinch

E

ENNISKILLEN BRANCH LIBRARY
Hallis Lane
ENNISKILLEN, BT74 7DR

TELEPHONE: 01365–322886; FAX: 01365–324685;
E-MAIL: branch@eknlib.demon.co.uk

HOURS:
MON, WED, FRI: 9:15 am–5:15 pm;
TUE, TH: 9:15 am–7:30 pm;
SAT: 9:15 am–1:00 pm

ACCESS:
Visitors welcome, but identification required. Borrowing
privileges for visitors may be restricted. Consult with
Librarian. About 85% of the collection catalogued on
cards, with 10% in machine readable form. Handicapped
accessible.

CONTACT PERSON: Margaret Kane, Assistant Librarian for
Local Studies

DESCRIPTION:
Library houses some 10,000 volumes, with a good local
history collection emphasizing Co. Fermanagh.

SPECIAL COLLECTIONS:
Nawn Collection on Irish and local history. Also
collections on W. B. Yeats, Fermanagh author Shan
Bullock, and military history. Holds microfilm copy of
1901 census for Co. Fermanagh.

SERVICES:
Photocopying, microfilm reader; nearby public car park.

SEE ALSO: WESTERN EDUCATION AND LIBRARY BOARD,
Omagh

ENNISKILLEN CASTLE
Castle Barracks
ENNISKILLEN, BT74 7HL

TELEPHONE: 01365–325000

HOURS:
MAY–SEPTEMBER: MON, SAT: 2:00 pm–5:00 pm;
TUE–FRI: 10:00 am–5:00 pm;

SUN: 2:00 pm–5:00 pm July and August only;
OCTOBER–APRIL: Closed Saturdays

ACCESS:
Open to general public. Admission charged. Current
fees: Adult = £2.00; Child = £1.00; special group,
family, student, and senior rates available. Partially
handicapped accessible.

CONTACT PERSON: Manager

DESCRIPTION:
Impressive castle on the banks of the River Erne. Houses
exhibits relating to the Castle and the museum of the
Royal Inniskilling Fusiliers. Also houses a new Heritage
Centre featuring exhibitions on the local landscape,
archaeology and history of Fermanagh.

SERVICES:
Craft and book shop, children's corner; special
exhibitions.

SEE ALSO:
ARMAGH COUNTY MUSEUM, Armagh; CAVAN COUNTY
MUSEUM, Ballyjamesduff; ULSTER MUSEUM, Belfast;
NORTH DOWN HERITAGE CENTRE, Bangor; ULSTER FOLK AND
TRANSPORT MUSEUM, Cultra; TOWER MUSEUM, Derry;
DOWN COUNTY MUSEUM; Downpatrick; DONEGAL COUNTY
MUSEUM, Letterkenny; IRISH LINEN CENTRE AND LISBURN
MUSEUM, Lisburn; MONAGHAN COUNTY MUSEUM,
Monaghan; and ULSTER-AMERICAN FOLK PARK, Omagh.

F

FINTONA BRANCH LIBRARY
112-114 Main Street
FINTONA, BT78 2BY

TELEPHONE: 01662–841774

HOURS:
MON: 2:00 pm–5:30 pm;
TUE: 12:00 pm–8:00 pm;
TH–FRI: 10:00 am–1:00 pm, 2:00 pm–5:30 pm;
SAT: 10:00 am–1:00 pm

ACCESS:
Visitors welcome, but identification required. Borrowing privileges for visitors may be restricted. Consult with Librarian.

CONTACT PERSON: Mrs. A. McCusker

SEE ALSO: WESTERN EDUCATION AND LIBRARY BOARD, Omagh

FIVEMILETOWN BRANCH LIBRARY
Main Street
FIVEMILETOWN, BT75 0PG

TELEPHONE: 013655–21409

HOURS:
TUE, TH: 11:00 am–1:30 pm, 2:00 pm–8:00 pm;
FRI: 11:00 am–1:30 pm, 2:00 pm–5:30 pm;
SAT: 11:00 am–1:30 pm, 2:00 pm–5:00 pm

ACCESS:
Visitors welcome, but identification required. Borrowing privileges for visitors may be restricted. Consult with Librarian.

CONTACT PERSON: Mrs. C. Daly-Finnegan

SEE ALSO: SOUTHERN EDUCATION AND LIBRARY BOARD, Armagh

GAOTH DOBHAIR
SEE DONEGAL COUNTY LIBRARY ADMINISTRATIVE CENTRE,
Letterkenny

GARVAGH BRANCH LIBRARY
Bridge Street
GARVAGH, BT51 5AF

TELEPHONE: 012665–58500

HOURS:
TUE: 10:00 am–1:30 pm, 2:00 pm–5:30 pm;
WED: 2:00 pm–4:00 pm;
FRI: 10:00 am–1:00 pm, 2:00 pm–5:00 pm, 5:30 pm–7:00
pm;
SAT: 10:00 am–1:30 pm, 2:00 pm–5:00 pm

ACCESS:
Visitors welcome, but identification required. Borrowing
privileges for visitors may be restricted. Consult with
Librarian.

CONTACT PERSON: Mrs. E. Murphy, Senior Library
Assistant in charge

SEE ALSO: NORTH EASTERN EDUCATION AND LIBRARY
BOARD, Ballymena

GILFORD BRANCH LIBRARY
Main Street
GILFORD, BT63 6HY

TELEPHONE: 01762–831770

HOURS:
MON, TUE: 2:00 pm–5:30 pm;
WED: 10:00 am–1:00 pm, 2:00 pm–8:00 pm;
FRI: 10:00–1:00 pm, 2:00 pm–5:30 pm;
SAT: 10:00 am–1:00 pm

ACCESS:
Visitors welcome, but identification required. Borrowing
privileges for visitors may be restricted. Consult with
Librarian.

CONTACT PERSON: Mrs. L. Wilson

SEE ALSO: SOUTHERN EDUCATION AND LIBRARY BOARD,
Armagh

GLENTIES BRANCH LIBRARY
SEE DONEGAL COUNTY LIBRARY ADMINISTRATIVE CENTRE,
Letterkenny

GREENISLAND BRANCH LIBRARY
17 Glassillan Grove
GREENISLAND, BT38 8PE

TELEPHONE: 01232–865419

HOURS:
MON, TH: 10:00 am–1:00 pm, 2:00 pm–5:30 pm;
TUE, FRI: 10:00 am–1:00 pm, 2:00 pm–8:00 pm;
SAT: 10:00 am–1:00 pm, 2:00 pm–5:00 pm

ACCESS:
Visitors welcome, but identification required. Borrowing
privileges for visitors may be restricted. Consult with
Librarian.

CONTACT PERSON: Mrs. W. Waite, Principal Library
Assistant in charge

SEE ALSO: NORTH EASTERN EDUCATION AND LIBRARY BOARD,
Ballymena

GREYSTONE BRANCH LIBRARY
SEE UNDER Antrim

HOLYWOOD BRANCH LIBRARY
Sullivan Building, 86-88 High Street
HOLYWOOD, BT18 9AE

TELEPHONE: 01232–424232; FAX: 01232–424194

HOURS:
MON, TUE, TH: 10:00 am–8:00 pm;
FRI: 10:00 am–5:00 pm;
SAT: 9:00 am–1:00 pm

ACCESS:
Visitors welcome, but identification required. Borrowing
privileges for visitors may be restricted. Consult with
Librarian. Handicapped accessible. Disabled parking.

CONTACT PERSON: Ms. Sharon Gregg, Branch Librarian

DESCRIPTION:
Attractive, inviting facility housed in a renovated 1862
building. Good reference collection on local history.
Book collection of some 21,000 volumes.

SERVICES:
Photocopying; microfilm reader; video rentals; nearby
public car park.

SEE ALSO: SOUTH EASTERN EDUCATION AND LIBRARY BOARD,
Ballynahinch

ULSTER FOLK AND TRANSPORT MUSEUM
SEE UNDER Cultra

I

IRVINESTOWN BRANCH LIBRARY
Main Street
IRVINESTOWN, BT94 1GT

TELEPHONE: 013656–21383

HOURS:
MON, TUE, FRI: 10:00 am–5:30 pm;
WED: 10:00 am– 7:30 pm;
SAT: 10:00 am–1:00 pm

ACCESS:
Visitors welcome, but identification required. Borrowing privileges for visitors may be restricted. Consult with Librarian.

CONTACT PERSON: Mrs. I. Hetherington

SEE ALSO
WESTERN EDUCATION AND LIBRARY BOARD, Omagh

UNIVERSITY OF ULSTER AT JORDANSTOWN
Shore Road
JORDANSTOWN, NEWTOWNABBEY, BT37 0QB

TELEPHONE: 01232–366370; FAX: 01232–366849
E–MAIL: dc.shorley@ulst.ac.uk

HOURS:
TERM: MON–FR: 9:00 am–10:00 pm;
SAT: 10:00 am–5:00 pm;
VACATION: MON–TH: 9:00 am–5:00 pm;
FRI: 9:00 am–4:00 pm

ACCESS:
Publicly-funded University library, part of the four-campus University of Ulster system, open to the public for reference purposes. Visitors welcome, but identification required. Borrowing privileges may be restricted. Consult with Librarian. Collection catalogued in machine readable form. Handicapped accessible.

CONTACT PERSON: Deborah Shorley, Pro Librarian

DESCRIPTION:
Largest of the four-campus University of Ulster system, Jordanstown is located just north of Belfast along the coastal road. Its library houses some 250,000 volumes, with special strengths in the areas of American and Women's studies. The total number of volumes for the four-campus system exceeds 600,000.

SPECIAL COLLECTIONS:
UK, USA and Irish radical newspapers and periodicals on microfilm.

SERVICES:
Photocopying; database searching; microfilm/fiche/reader/printer; brochures; finding aids; free parking by prior arrangement

SEE ALSO:
UNIVERSITY OF ULSTER AT BELFAST, Belfast; UNIVERSITY OF ULSTER AT COLERAINE, Coleraine; and UNIVERSITY OF ULSTER, MAGEE COLLEGE, Derry.

KEADY BRANCH LIBRARY
Market Street
KEADY, BT60 3RP

TELEPHONE: 01861–531365

HOURS:
MON, FRI: 10:00 am–6:00 pm;
WED: 10:00 am–8:00 pm;
SAT: 10:00 am–5:00 pm

ACCESS:
Visitors welcome, but identification required. Borrowing
privileges for visitors may be restricted. Consult with
Librarian.

CONTACT PERSON: Mrs. F. Toner

SEE ALSO: SOUTHERN EDUCATION AND LIBRARY BOARD,
Armagh

KILKEEL BRANCH LIBRARY
Greencastle Street
KILKEEL, BT34 4BH

TELEPHONE: 016937–62278

HOURS:
MON, WED, FRI: 10:00 am–5:30 pm;
TUE: 10:00 am–8:00 pm;
SAT: 10:00 am–5:00 pm

ACCESS:
Visitors welcome, but identification required. Borrowing
privileges for visitors may be restricted. Consult with
Librarian.

CONTACT PERSON: Mrs. E. Colgan

SEE ALSO: SOUTHERN EDUCATION AND LIBRARY BOARD,
Armagh

KILLESHANDRA BRANCH LIBRARY
SEE CAVAN COUNTY COUNCIL BRANCH LIBRARIES, Cavan

KILLYBEGS BRANCH LIBRARY
SEE DONEGAL COUNTY LIBRARY ADMINISTRATIVE CENTRE,
Letterkenny

KILLYLEAGH BRANCH LIBRARY
High Street
KILLYLEAGH, DOWNPATRICK, BT30 9QF

TELEPHONE: 01396–828407

HOURS:
MON, WED: 2:00 pm–8:00 pm;
FRI: 10:00 am–1:00 pm, 2:00 pm–5:00 pm;
SAT: 10:00 am–1:00 pm

ACCESS:
Visitors welcome, but identification required. Borrowing
privileges for visitors may be restricted. Consult with
Librarian.

CONTACT PERSON: Mrs. Bridget Napier, Branch Librarian

SEE ALSO: SOUTH EASTERN EDUCATION AND LIBRARY BOARD,
Ballynahinch

KILNALECK BRANCH LIBRARY
SEE CAVAN COUNTY COUNCIL BRANCH LIBRARIES, Cavan

KILREA BRANCH LIBRARY
Town Hall, 27 The Diamond
KILREA, BT51 5QN

TELEPHONE: 012665–40630

HOURS:
TUE, WED, FRI: 10:30 am–1:00 pm, 2:00 pm–5:30 pm;
SAT: 10:00 am–1:00 pm; 2:00 pm–5:00 pm

ACCESS:
Visitors welcome, but identification required. Borrowing
privileges for visitors may be restricted. Consult with
Librarian.

CONTACT PERSON: Mrs. R. Kirkpatrick, Senior Library
Assistant in charge

SEE ALSO: NORTH EASTERN EDUCATION AND LIBRARY
BOARD, Ballymena

KINGSCOURT BRANCH LIBRARY
SEE CAVAN COUNTY COUNCIL BRANCH LIBRARIES, Cavan

L

LARNE BRANCH LIBRARY
36 Pound Street
LARNE, BT40 1SQ

TELEPHONE: 01574–277047

HOURS:
MON, TH: 10:00 am–8:00 pm;
TUE, WED, FRI: 10:00 am–5:30 pm;
SAT: 10:00 am–5:00 pm

ACCESS:
Visitors welcome, but identification required. Borrowing
privileges for visitors may be restricted. Consult with
Librarian.

CONTACT PERSON: Mrs. P. McAuley, Principal Library
Assistant in charge

SEE ALSO: NORTH EASTERN EDUCATION AND LIBRARY BOARD,
Ballymena

DONEGAL COUNTY LIBRARY
CENTRAL LIBRARY AND ARTS CENTRE
Oliver Plunkett Road
LETTERKENNY, COUNTY DONEGAL

TELEPHONE: 074–24950; FAX: 074–24959;
E–MAIL: dglcolib.iol.ie

HOURS:
MON, WED, FRI: 10:30 am–5:30 pm;
TUE, TH: 10:30 am–8:00 pm;
SAT: 10:30 am–1:00 pm

ACCESS:
Visitors welcome. Borrowing privileges available.
Collection catalogued in machine readable form, using
Genesis System. Handicapped accessible.

CONTACT PERSON: Noreen O'Neill, Assistant Librarian

DESCRIPTION:
Central library is the heart of the County Library service.
This library houses 35,000 of the some 300,000 volumes
in the system. The system also holds 185 periodical
titles, plus videos, microfilm, photos, maps, newspapers,
prints and some manuscripts.

SPECIAL COLLECTIONS:
Papers of Patrick McGill, Seamus MacManus, and John
Kells Ingram. There is also a modest collection of pre-
1851 printed books and an important Donegal studies
collection. The latter covers the history, archaeology,
natural history, literature and culture of Donegal.

SERVICES:
Photocopying; exhibitions; brochures.

DONEGAL COUNTY LIBRARY
ADMINISTRATIVE CENTRE
Rosemount
LETTERKENNY, COUNTY DONEGAL

TELEPHONE: 074–21968; FAX: 074–26402;
E–MAIL: dglcolib.iol.ie

HOURS:
MON–FRI: 9:00 am–4:30 pm

ACCESS:
By appointment

CONTACT PERSON: Liam O Ronain, County Librarian

DESCRIPTION:
Administrative headquarters for the County Library
System. In addition to the Central Library, Letterkenny,
the County System includes 15 branch libraries. Visitors
are welcome, but please note all these branch libraries
operate on a part-ime basis. Branch libraries below are
arranged by district: Fanad/Lagan, Inis Eoghain, South
Donegal, and the Gaeltacht.

FANAD/LAGAN:
BALLYBOFEY: Butt Hall, Ballybofey.

TELEPHONE: 074–31822

HOURS: WED, SAT: 4:00 pm–6:00 pm;
SUN: 11:00 am–1:00 pm

CONTACT PERSON: Mrs. Eileen Harkin

LIFFORD COMMUNITY: Courthouse, Lifford

TELEPHONE: 074–41066

HOURS:
MON: 3:00 pm–7:00 pm;
TUE, TH: 3:00 pm–8:30 pm;
FRI: 10:00 am–1:00 pm, 3:00 pm–7:00 pm

CONTACT PERSON: Ms. Jane Friel

MILFORD: Main Street, Milford

TELEPHONE: 074–41066

HOURS:
MON, SAT: 4:00 pm–6:00 pm;
TH: 3:00 pm–5:30 pm

CONTACT PERSON: Ms. Helen McNutt

RAMELTON COMMUNITY: Old Meetinghouse, Ramelton

TELEPHONE: 074–51414

HOURS:
MON, WED: 3:00 pm–8:30 pm;
FRI: 10:00 am–1:00 pm, 3:00 pm–7:00 pm;
SAT: 3:00 pm–7:00 pm

CONTACT PERSON: Ms. Phyllis Loughrey (temp)

RAPHOE: Diamond, Raphoe

TELEPHONE: NA

HOURS:
WED: 3:00 pm–4:30 pm;
SAT: 3:30 pm–5:30 pm;
SUN: 11:30 am–1:00 pm

CONTACT PERSON: Ms. Rita Gallagher

INIS EOGHAIN:
BUNCRANA: Courthouse, Buncrana

TELEPHONE: NA

HOURS:
MON, FRI: 4:00 pm–6:00 pm;
WED: 6:30 pm–8:30 pm;
SUN: 11:00 am–1:30 pm

CONTACT PERSON: Ms. Nina Quigley

CARDONAGH: Courthouse, Cardonagh

TELEPHONE: NA

HOURS:
WED: 3:30 pm–5:00 pm;
SAT: 7:00 pm–9:00 pm;
SUN: 12:00 pm–1:00 pm

CONTACT PERSON: Ms. Anna Hegarty

CLONMANY: Parochial Hall, Clonmany

TELEPHONE: NA

HOURS:
WED, TH: 3:00 pm–5:00 pm;
SUN: 12:00 pm–1:00 pm

CONTACT PERSON: Ms.Nell Lavelle

MOVILLE: St. Eugene's Hall, Moville

TELEPHONE: NA

HOURS:
TU, TH, SAT: 3:00 pm–5:00 pm;
WED: 6:30 pm–8:30 pm

CONTACT PERSON: Ms.Carmel Barron

SOUTH DONEGAL:
BALLYSHANNON: Credit Union, East Port, Ballyshannon

TELEPHONE: NA

HOURS:
MON: 7:00 pm–9:00 pm;
WED: 6:30 pm–8:30 pm

CONTACT PERSON: Ms.Carmel Barron

BUNDORAN: UDC Offices, Main Street, Bundoran

TELEPHONE: NA

HOURS:
MON, WED, FRI: 2:00 pm–5:00 pm

CONTACT PERSON: Ms. Jill O'Doherty

DONEGAL: Mountcharles Road, Donegal

TELEPHONE: NA

HOURS:
MON, WED, FRI: 3:00 pm–6:00 pm;
SAT: 11:00 am–1:00 pm, 2:00 pm–6:00 pm

CONTACT PERSON: Ms. Rita Kerrigan

GLENTIES: Courthouse, Glenties

TELEPHONE: NA

HOURS:
TUE, TH: 3:00 pm–6:00 pm;
SAT: 11:00 am–1:00 pm, 2:00 pm–6:00 pm

CONTACT PERSON: Ms. Rita Kerrigan

KILLYBEGS: Bruach na Mara, Killybegs

TELEPHONE: NA

HOURS:
MON: 5:30 pm–7:30 pm;
WED, FRI: 7:00 pm–9:00 pm

CONTACT PERSON: Ms. Sylvia Murrin

GAELTACHT:
GAOTH DOBHAIR: Sean tSeipeal, Gaoth Dobhair

TELEPHONE: NA

HOURS:
MON, SAT: 3:00 pm–6:00 pm;
WED: 3:00 pm–6:00 pm, 6:30 pm–8:00 pm;
FRI: 10:00 am–1:00 pm, 3:00 pm–6:00 pm

CONTACT PERSON: Maire Bean ui Bhaoill

DONEGAL COUNTY MUSEUM
High Road
LETTERKENNY, COUNTY DONEGAL

TELEPHONE: 074–24613; FAX: 074–26522

HOURS:
MON–FRI: 10:00 am–12:30 pm, 1:00 pm–4:30 pm;
SAT: 1:00 pm–4:30 pm

ACCESS:
Publicly-funded museum whose archive and exhibits are
open to public free of charge. Advance notification by
letter preferred for permission to use archives collection,
which is not catalogued. About 90% of the artefact
collection is catalogued. Handicapped accessible.

CONTACT PERSON: Judith McCarthy, Curator

DESCRIPTION:
Donegal County Museum was opened in 1987 in the
renovated Letterkenny workhouse, which operated from
1843 to 1922. The museum collects, preserves and
displays the material heritage of County Donegal. The
collection currently includes some 8,000 artefacts, some

dating back to the Stone Age, plus some archival collections.

SPECIAL COLLECTIONS:
Records from Lough Swilly Bus & Rail Company (Londonderry & Lough Swilly Bus & Rail Company) for early part of the 20th century. Also some local photographs.

SERVICES:
Photocopying; exhibitions, both permanent and temporary; car parking but no coach parking.

SEE ALSO:
ARMAGH COUNTY MUSEUM; Armagh; CAVAN COUNTY MUSEUM, Ballyjamesduff; NORTH DOWN HERITAGE CENTRE, Bangor; ULSTER MUSEUM, Belfast; TOWER MUSEUM, Derry; DOWN COUNTY MUSEUM; Downpatrick; ENNISKILLEN CASTLE, Enniskillen; ULSTER FOLK AND TRANSPORT MUSEUM, Cultra; IRISH LINEN CENTRE AND LISBURN MUSEUM, Lisburn; MONAGHAN COUNTY MUSEUM, Monaghan; and ULSTER-AMERICAN FOLK PARK, Omagh.

THE GLEBE HOUSE AND GALLERY
Church Hill
LETTERKENNY, COUNTY DONEGAL

TELEPHONE: 074–37071; FAX: 074–37072

HOURS:
MID–MAY–OCTOBER: SAT,–TH: 11:00 am–6:00 pm; Closed Fridays. Open Easter Sunday.

ACCESS:
The House and Gallery are operated by the Heritage Service of the Irish Department of Arts, Culture and Gaeltacht, and are open to the public for an admission charge. Current fees: Adult = £2; Seniors £1.50; Children and Students = £1. Family rate also available. Handicapped accessible.

CONTACT PERSON: Mr. Chris Wilson, Supervisor

DESCRIPTION:
Glebe House and Gallery contain the Derek Hill Collection of paintings, furniture, textiles and objects d'art given to the state in 1983. There are 310 paintings in the collection. In addition to many of Hill's own paintings, the Gallery and House feature works by leading twentieth century artists, including Picasso. The

Regency house is furnished and decorated with
Victoriana, William Morris paper and textiles, and
various twentieth-century paintings, including Tory
Island primitives.

SPECIAL COLLECTIONS:
Derek Hill Paintings, Twentieth Century European
Paintings, William Morris Papers and Textiles; Islamic
Art; Japanese Prints and Donegal Primitive Painters
(Tory Island).

SERVICES:
Ample parking; brochures, booklets; shop; guided tours.

CAVANACOR HISTORIC HOUSE & CRAFT CENTRE
Ballindrait
LIFFORD, COUNTY DONEGAL

TELEPHONE: 074–41143; FAX: 074–41143

HOURS:
EASTER–SEPTEMBER: TUE–SAT: 12:00 pm–6:00 pm;
SUN: 2:00 pm–6:00 pm;
Open Monday bank holidays only.

ACCESS:
Ancestral home of James Knox Polk, 11th President of
the United States (1845-1849), Cavanacor is open
seasonally to the public for an admission charge. Current
fees: Adult = £2.50; Children and Seniors = £1.50.
Group rates available. Limited handicapped
accessibility.

CONTACT PERSON: Joanna O'Kane, Manager

DESCRIPTION:
Seventeenth-century ancestral home of President Polk,
Cavanacor is one of the oldest inhabited houses in
Donegal. It once entertained King James II in 1689 at the
time of the Siege of Derry. It contains a museum
detailing the history of President Polk and the visit of
King James II. There is also a tea room, a craft shop, a
pottery and a museum and gallery exhibiting
contemporary painting and sculpture on the grounds. The
gallery features the art work of Joanna and Eddie
O'Kane. The 10-acre site also boasts a 300-year old
garden. Some research materials on the history of the
house and the area available for reference purposes only.

SERVICES:
Parking, shop, exhibitions.

LIFFORD COMMUNITY BRANCH LIBRARY

SEE DONEGAL COUNTY LIBRARY ADMINISTRATIVE CENTRE,
Letterkenny

LIFFORD OLD COURTHOUSE VISITORS CENTRE

The Diamond
LIFFORD, COUNTY DONEGAL

TELEPHONE: 074–41733; FAX: 074–41754

HOURS:
MARCH 17–OCTOBER 31: MON–SAT: 10:00 am–6:00 pm;
SUN: 2:00 pm–6:00 pm

ACCESS:
Open to the public for an admission charge. Current
fees: Adult = £3.00. Limited handicapped access.

CONTACT PERSON: Sheena Clifford, Manager

DESCRIPTION:
The Old Courthouse was built in 1746 by Dublin
architect Michael Priestly and functioned as a
courthouse until 1938. It was restored and reopened as a
Heritage Centre in 1994. It traces the history of Lifford,
especially its struggle for "seat of power" in Donegal,
and the history of the O'Donnell dynasty, using audio-
visual aids and displays. Lifford was also the
administrative centre for the Plantation. The building is
believed to have been built on the foundation of Lifford
Castle, a sixteenth- and seventeenth-century O'Donnell
stronghold.

SPECIAL COLLECTIONS:
Rupert Coughlan Collection of documents, manuscripts
and charts on the O'Donnell Clan. Also, archive houses
artefacts, letters, photographs, and minute books, the
latter dating back to Famine days.

SERVICES:
Exhibitions; brochures; genealogical research service,
with special attention to the O'Donnell family.

IRISH LINEN CENTRE AND LISBURN MUSEUM

Market Square
LISBURN, BT28 1AG

TELEPHONE: 01846–663377; FAX: 01846–672624

HOURS:
APRIL–SEPTEMBER: MON–SAT: 9:30 am–5:30 pm;
SUN: 2:00 pm–5:30 pm;
OCTOBER–MARCH: MON–SAT: 9:30 am–5:00 pm

ACCESS:
Open to the general public. Admission charged. Current
fees: Adult = £2.75; Children under 17, Students,
Seniors, Unemployed = £1.75; group and family rates
available

CONTACT PERSON: Museum Manager

DESCRIPTION:
New museum traces the historical development of
Ireland's linen industry from its origins to the present.
Exhibition "Flax to Fabric" features weaving workshop.
Adjoining textile gallery exhibits museum's collection of
linen damask cloth.

SERVICES:
Exhibitions, linen shop; cafe.

SEE ALSO:
ARMAGH COUNTY MUSEUM, Armagh; CAVAN COUNTY
MUSEUM, Ballyjamesduff; NORTH DOWN HERITAGE
CENTRE, Bangor; ULSTER MUSEUM, Belfast; TOWER
MUSEUM, Derry; DOWN COUNTY MUSEUM; Downpatrick;
ENNISKILLEN CASTLE, Enniskillen; ULSTER FOLK AND
TRANSPORT MUSEUM, Cultra; DONEGAL COUNTY MUSEUM,
Letterkenny; MONAGHAN COUNTY MUSEUM, Monaghan;
and ULSTER-AMERICAN FOLK PARK, Omagh.

LAURELHILL COMMUNITY LIBRARY
Laurelhill Road
LISBURN, BT28 2UH

TELEPHONE: 01846–664596

HOURS:
MON: 10:00 am–1:00 pm, 2:00 pm–6:00 pm;
TUE, TH: 2:00 pm–8:00 pm;
WED, FRI: 2:00 pm–6:00 pm;
SAT: 10:00 am–1:00 pm

ACCESS:
Visitors welcome, but identification required. Borrowing
privileges for visitors may be restricted. Consult with
Librarian. CD-ROM-based catalogue access to other NI
public library systems available as well. Collection strong
on National Curriculum subjects. Handicapped accessible.

CONTACT PERSON: Mr. Michael Bell, Branch Librarian

SEE ALSO: SOUTH EASTERN EDUCATION AND LIBRARY BOARD,
Ballynahinch

LISBURN BRANCH LIBRARY
29 Railway Street
LISBURN, BT28 1XP

TELEPHONE: 01846–601749

HOURS:
MON–FR: 10:00 am–8:00 pm;
Closed Wed;
SAT: 10:00 am–1:00 pm, 2:00 pm–5:00 pm

ACCESS:
Visitors welcome, but identification required. Borrowing
privileges for visitors may be restricted. Consult with
Librarian. Limited accessibility for handicapped.
Collection catalogued in machine readable form.

CONTACT PERSON: Mrs. Margaret Bell, Branch Librarian

DESCRIPTION:
Multi-purpose library of some 29,000 volumes, with a
good collection of videos, cassettes, CDs, and music
scores. Serves both an urban and a rural population.

SERVICES:
Photocopying; finding aids; brochures; public car park
nearby.

SEE ALSO: SOUTH EASTERN EDUCATION AND LIBRARY BOARD,
Ballynahinch

LIMAVADY BRANCH LIBRARY
5 Connell Street
LIMAVADY, BT49 0EA

TELEPHONE: 01504–762540

HOURS:
MON: 1:00 pm–7:30 pm;
TUE, TH, FRI: 9:15 am–5:30 pm;
WED: 9:15 am–7:30 pm;
SAT: 9:15 am–1:00 pm

ACCESS:
Visitors welcome, but identification required. Borrowing

privileges for visitors may be restricted. Consult with Librarian.

CONTACT PERSON: Mr. Liam Kennedy

SEE ALSO: WESTERN EDUCATION AND LIBRARY BOARD, Omagh

LISNASKEA BRANCH LIBRARY
Drumhaw
LISNASKEA, BT92 0FC

TELEPHONE: 013657–21222

HOURS:
MON, TUE, FRI: 10:00 am–5:30 pm;
WED: 10:00 am–7:30 pm;
SAT: 10:00 am–1:00 pm

ACCESS:
Visitors welcome, but identification required. Borrowing privileges for visitors may be restricted. Consult with Librarian.

CONTACT PERSON: Position open

SEE ALSO: WESTERN EDUCATION AND LIBRARY BOARD, Omagh

LONDONDERRY, SEE Derry

LURGAN BRANCH LIBRARY
Carnegie Street
LURGAN, BT66 6AS

TELEPHONE: 01762–323912

HOURS:
MON, FRI: 10:00 am–5:30 pm;
TUE, TH: 10:00 am–8:00 pm;
WED, SAT: 10:00 am–5:00 pm

ACCESS:
Visitors welcome, but identification required. Borrowing privileges for visitors may be restricted. Consult with Librarian.

CONTACT PERSON: Mrs. M. McNeill

SEE ALSO: SOUTHERN EDUCATION AND LIBRARY BOARD, Armagh

MAGHERA BRANCH LIBRARY
1 Main Street
MAGHERA, BT46 5EA

TELEPHONE: 01648–42578

HOURS:
MON, WED–FRI: 10:00 am–5:30 pm;
TUE: 10:00 am–7:30 pm;
SAT: 10:00 am–5:00 pm

ACCESS:
Visitors welcome, but identification required. Borrowing
privileges for visitors may be restricted. Consult with
Librarian.

CONTACT PERSON: Mrs. L. O'Neill, Senior Library
Assistant in charge

SEE ALSO: NORTH EASTERN EDUCATION AND LIBRARY
BOARD, Ballymena

MAGHERAFELT BRANCH LIBRARY
43 Queen's Avenue
MAGHERAFELT, BT45 6BX

TELEPHONE: 01648–32278

HOURS:
MON–SAT: 10:00 am–1:00 pm, 2:00 pm–5:00 pm;
EXCEPT TH: 1:00 pm–5:00 pm, 6:00 pm–8:00 pm

ACCESS:
Visitors welcome, but identification required. Borrowing
privileges for visitors may be restricted. Consult with
Librarian.

CONTACT PERSON: Mrs. A. Wilson, Senior Library
Assistant in charge

SEE ALSO: NORTH EASTERN EDUCATION AND LIBRARY
BOARD, Ballymena

MILFORD BRANCH LIBRARY
SEE DONEGAL COUNTY LIBRARY ADMINISTRATIVE CENTRE,
Letterkenny

MOIRA LIBRARY
SEE UNDER Craigavon

THE HERITAGE CENTRE
St. Louis Convent
MONAGHAN, COUNTY MONAGHAN

TELEPHONE: 047–83529

HOURS:
MON, TUE, TH, FRI: 10:00 am–12:00 pm, 2:30 pm–4:30 pm;
SAT, SUN: 2:30 pm–4:30 pm

ACCESS:
Privately-funded heritage centre open to the public for a
modest admission fee. Current fees: Adults = £1;
Children = 50p. Handicapped accessible.

CONTACT PERSON: Sister Mona Lally, Director

DESCRIPTION:
The heritage centre is dedicated to the conservation and
preservation of the historical, artistic and cultural
heritage of the St. Louis Sisters, a Catholic religious
order of women founded in France in 1842. The origins
of the community date back to the end of the French
Revolution, however. The centre is located on the
grounds of the Monaghan convent, founded in 1859 by
Mother Genevieve Beale (1820-1878). The centre's
permanent exhibition features documents, books,
artefacts, crafts, newspapers, paintings, tapestries, and
photographs tracing the history of the St. Louis women
and their work. The Sisters have been an integral part of
County Monaghan and surrounding areas for a century
and a half, and the exhibit documents not only their lives
but the life of this broader community, especially its
social, educational and religious heritage. The exhibit
also features documents and photographs from from its
overseas missions, including the schools in California
operated by the Sisters. The Sisters formerly operated an
orphanage and a residential school on the grounds, and
continue to operate a day school there.

SPECIAL COLLECTIONS:
Photographs, documents, liturgical and devotional items,
crafts, including 19th century Belleek China, antiques,
and archival material, including records of members of
the religious community, students and orphans. Records
may be restricted. Consult with director.

SERVICES:
Exhibitions, both permanent and temporary; free
parking.

MONAGHAN ANCESTRY
6 Tully
MONAGHAN, CO. MONAGHAN

TELEPHONE: O47–82304; FAX: SAME;
E-MAIL: theo@tinet.ie

HOURS:
MON–FRI: 10:00 am–5:30 pm
By appointment only

ACCESS:
Privately-funded ancestral research organization located
in a private home. The Centre prefers to deal with postal
enquiries only. Fees are charged.

CONTACT PERSON: Theo McMahon or Maire O'Neill

DESCRIPTION:
Monaghan Ancestry is a branch of the Clogher Historical
Society and a member of the Irish Genealogical Project.
It deals specifically with Co. Monaghan ancestry. To
date it has computerized more than half the county's
parish records and this project is ongoing. Its
genealogical resources for the county are many and
varied and include all Catholic baptismal and marriage
records from their commencement up to and including
1880. Other sources include Tithe Applotment Books for
22 of the 23 civil parishes. Only one parish, Tydavnet,
does not have a detailed return in this series. Other
records include the Griffith Primary Valuations of the
1858-1861 period; the 1901 Census for County
Monaghan; gravestone inscriptions of locations already
recorded; IGI 1988 and 1992; Royal Irish Constabulary
records, 1816-1921; civil records (non Roman Catholic)
of marriages from 1845 to 1900 for most parishes; Old
Age Pension Claims, some with extracts from the 1841
and the 1851 Census.

Monaghan Ancestry also holds 1901 census data for
Counties Fermanagh and Tyrone, as some of the Co.
Monaghan parishes are contiguous to these counties.
Other items include rentals of the Rose Estate,
Tydavnet, 1839-1847 (these replace to some degree the
loss of the Tithe Applotment Book for certain townlands
in this parish); the Templetown Estate (mostly in

Muckno parish) for 1805; the Forster Estate Rentals for certain townlands 1802-1808; the Murray Ker Estate (Killeevan/Newbliss), 1881-1911 and 1937; Rentals of the Kane Estate 1764; the Famine Relief Books for Donagh and Errigal Truagh parishes by townland, January-May 1847; Donaghmoyne Vaccination Register, 1869-1884; Index to Clogher Wills, 1659-1857; Lennard Barrett Estate Records and Rentals for Clones, 1682-1845, etc. In addition, the Reference Collection consists of all publications of the Clogher Historical Society, 1953-1996 inclusive.

SERVICES:
Genealogical searches are made for fees ranging from £10 to £100. Estimates of costs are made based on the availability of records and the estimated time involved in preparing a report and the format in which the information is required.

PUBLICATIONS:
Monaghan Ancestry has been editing and publishing the annual *Clogher Record*, the journal of the Clogher Historical Society since 1975. Clogher Diocese covers Counties Monaghan, Fermanagh, south Tyrone and a small portion of Co. Donegal around Bundoran and Ballyshannon. The journal, issued worldwide, is devoted to the religious, social, economic, genealogical, archaeological and political history of the diocese. Other publications include *Old Monaghan 1785-1995,* a history of Monaghan Town, and the reintroduction of Denis Carolan Rushe's *History of Monaghan for Two Hundred Years, 1660-1860.* James H. Murnane's and Peadar Murnane's *History of Ballybay* is scheduled for publication in late 1997.

SEE ALSO:
ARMAGH ANCESTRY, Armagh; ULSTER HISTORICAL FOUNDATION, Belfast; CAVAN GENEALOGICAL RESEARCH CENTRE, Cavan; THE GENEALOGY CENTRE, Derry; HERITAGE WORLD, Dungannon; and DONEGAL ANCESTRY, Ramelton;. ALSO: GENERAL REGISTER OFFICE, Belfast; and PUBLIC RECORD OFFICE OF NORTHERN IRELAND, Belfast.

MONAGHAN BRANCH LIBRARY
North Road
MONAGHAN, COUNTY MONAGHAN

TELEPHONE: 047-81830

HOURS:
MON, WED, FRI: 11:00 am–1:00 pm, 2:00 pm–5:00 pm,
6:00 pm–8:00 pm;
TUE, TH: 11:00 am–1:00 pm, 2:00 pm–5:00 pm

ACCESS:
Visitors welcome. Borrowing privileges are available to
visitors. There is a £2 annual fee for adults. Limited
handicapped access.

CONTACT PERSON: Mary McKenna, Senior Library
Assistant

DESCRIPTION:
Community-based library located in the town centre.

SPECIAL COLLECTIONS:
Small local history collection, plus an Irish collection of
general interest.

SEE ALSO: MONAGHAN COUNTY LIBRARY, Clones

MONAGHAN COUNTY MUSEUM
1-2 Hill Street
MONAGHAN, COUNTY MONAGHAN

TELEPHONE: 047–82928; FAX: 047–71189

HOURS:
TUE–FRI: 11:00 am–5:00 pm;
SAT: 11:00 am–1:00 pm, 2:00 pm–5:00 pm;
Closed from 1:00 pm–2:00 pm October–May.

ACCESS:
Publicly-funded museum open to the public free of
charge. Limited handicapped access. Museum is located
on a hillside.

CONTACT PERSON: Curator

DESCRIPTION:
Monaghan County Museum seeks to document the
material heritage of County Monaghan and the
surrounding area primarily through exhibitions of
artefacts and paintings. This award-winning (Council of
Europe Museum Prize, 1980) Museum was established
in 1974. It moved into its present quarters in 1986. The
Museum is distinguished for its presentation of material
dating from circa 5,000 BC to the present. Of special
interest is the Cross of Clogher, a fourteenth-century oak
cross decorated with bronze and semi-precious metals.

The Museum also houses a fine collection of early medieval crannog (lake dwelling) artefacts. Monaghan County Museum is paired with Old Sturbridge Village in Massachusetts.

SERVICES:
Exhibitions, both permanent and temporary; public car parks nearby.

SEE ALSO:
ARMAGH COUNTY MUSEUM; Armagh; CAVAN COUNTY MUSEUM, Ballyjamesduff; NORTH DOWN HERITAGE CENTRE, Bangor; ULSTER MUSEUM, Belfast; TOWER MUSEUM, Derry; DOWN COUNTY MUSEUM; Downpatrick; ENNISKILLEN CASTLE, Enniskillen; ULSTER FOLK AND TRANSPORT MUSEUM, Cultra; DONEGAL COUNTY MUSEUM, Letterkenny; IRISH LINEN CENTRE AND LISBURN MUSEUM, Lisburn; and ULSTER-AMERICAN FOLK PARK, Omagh.

MONEYMORE BRANCH LIBRARY
8 Main Street
MONEYMORE, BT45 7PD

TELEPHONE: 016487–48380

HOURS:
MON: 1:00 pm–6:00 pm;
TUE: 10:00 am–1:00 pm, 2:00 pm–6:00 pm;
FRI: 2:00 pm–6:00 pm;
SAT: 10:00 am–1:00 pm, 2:00 pm–5:00 pm

ACCESS:
Visitors welcome, but identification required. Borrowing privileges for visitors may be restricted. Consult with Librarian.
CONTACT PERSON: Mrs. E. Chambers

SEE ALSO: SOUTHERN EDUCATION AND LIBRARY BOARD, Armagh

MONKSTOWN BRANCH LIBRARY
Monkstown Secondary School, Bridge Road
MONKSTOWN, BT37 0EG

TELEPHONE: 01232–853138

HOURS:
MON, TUE: 1:30 pm–5:30 pm, 6:30–8:00 pm;
TH, FRI: 10:00 am–1:00 pm, 2:00 pm–5:30 pm

ACCESS:
Visitors welcome, but identification required. Borrowing privileges for visitors may be restricted. Consult with Librarian.

CONTACT PERSON: Mrs. C. Bradley, Senior Library Assistant in charge

SEE ALSO: NORTH EASTERN EDUCATION AND LIBRARY BOARD, Ballymena

MOVILLE BRANCH LIBRARY
SEE DONEGAL COUNTY LIBRARY ADMINISTRATIVE CENTRE, Letterkenny

MOY BRANCH LIBRARY
The Square
MOY, BT71 7SG

TELEPHONE: 01868–784661

HOURS:
TUE: 10:00 am–1:00 pm, 2:00 pm–5:30 pm;
WED: 2:00 pm–5:30 pm;
FRI: 2:00 pm– 8:00 pm;
SAT: 10:00 am–1:00 pm, 2:00 pm–5:00 pm

ACCESS:
Visitors welcome, but identification required. Borrowing privileges for visitors may be restricted. Consult with Librarian.

CONTACT PERSON: Mrs. E. Telford

SEE ALSO: SOUTHERN EDUCATION AND LIBRARY BOARD, Armagh

NEWCASTLE BRANCH LIBRARY
141/143 Main Street
NEWCASTLE, BT33 0AE

TELEPHONE: 013967–22710; FAX: 013967–26518

HOURS:
MON–WED: 10:00 am–8:00 pm;
FRI: 10:00 am–5:00 pm;
SAT: 10:00 am–1:00 pm, 2:00 pm–5:00 pm

ACCESS:
Visitors welcome, but identification required. Borrowing
privileges for visitors may be restricted. Consult with
Librarian. Handicapped accessible. Catalogue on CD
ROM.

CONTACT PERSON: Mrs. Valerie McIlroy, Temporary
Branch Librarian

DESCRIPTION:
Attractive, relatively new facility located beside the
Shimna Bridge on the main street in this popular seaside
resort town in South Down. General collection of about
10,000 volumes, plus recordings, videos and
newspapers. Community events publicized in the library.

SERVICES:
Photocopying; limited parking; fax; multi-media PC.

SEE ALSO: SOUTH EASTERN EDUCATION AND LIBRARY BOARD,
Ballynahinch

NEWRY BRANCH LIBRARY
79 Hill Street
NEWRY, BT34 1DG

TELEPHONE: 01693–64683; FAX: 01693–251739

HOURS:
MON, FRI: 9:30 am–6:00 pm;
TUE, TH: 9:30 am–8:00 pm;
WED, SAT: 9:30 am–5:00 pm

ACCESS:
Visitors welcome, but identification required. Borrowing
privileges for visitors may be restricted. Consult with

Librarian. Collection catalogued in machine readable form. Handicapped accessible.

CONTACT PERSON: Mrs. Christina Sloan, Branch Librarian

DESCRIPTION:
Attractive, relatively new library with a general collection of some 40,000 volumes, 1,000 videos, and more than 3,500 recordings. Strong reference collection.

SERVICES:
Photocopying; finding aids; microfilm reader/printer; nearby car park.

SEE ALSO: SOUTHERN EDUCATION AND LIBRARY BOARD, Armagh

NEWRY DIVISIONAL LIBRARY HEADQUARTERS
79 Hill Street
NEWRY, BT34 1DG

TELEPHONE: 01693–64077/61652; FAX: 01693–251739

HOURS:
MON–FRI: 9:00 am–5:00 pm

ACCESS:
By appointment

CONTACT PERSON: Miss J. Blair, Divisional Librarian

SEE ALSO: SOUTHERN EDUCATION AND LIBRARY BOARD, Armagh

SISTERS OF MERCY
Convent of Mercy
NEWRY, COUNTY DOWN

TELEPHONE: 01693–64964

HOURS:
Not applicable

ACCESS:
Enquiries by mail only

CONTACT PERSON: Archivist

DESCRIPTION:
Houses the archives of the Sisters of Mercy, Newry.

Includes material relating to the Newry convent and the general history of the Sister of Mercy Order.

CLOUGHFERN BRANCH LIBRARY
2a Kings Crescent
NEWTOWNABBEY, BT37 0DH

TELEPHONE: 01232–854789

HOURS:
MON, FRI: 2:00 pm–8:00 pm;
WED: 10:30 am–5:00 pm;
SAT: 10:30 am–1:00 pm

ACCESS:
Visitors welcome, but identification required. Borrowing privileges for visitors may be restricted. Consult with Librarian.

CONTACT PERSON: Mrs. I McCrea, Senior Library Assistant in charge

SEE ALSO: NORTH EASTERN EDUCATION AND LIBRARY BOARD, Ballymena

GLENGORMLEY BRANCH LIBRARY
40 Carnmoney Road
NEWTOWNABBEY, BT36 6HP

TELEPHONE: 01232–833797

HOURS:
MON, TUE: 10:00 am–5:30 pm;
WED-FRI: 10:00 am–8:00 pm;
SAT: 10:00 am–5:00 pm

ACCESS:
Visitors welcome, but identification required. Borrowing privileges for visitors may be restricted. Consult with Librarian. Collection catalogued in machine readable form, with computerized access to holdings of Queen's University and Linenhall Library. Handicapped accessible.

CONTACT PERSON: Mrs. A. Crane, District Librarian in charge

SEE ALSO: NORTH EASTERN EDUCATION AND LIBRARY BOARD, Ballymena

UNIVERSITY OF ULSTER AT JORDANSTOWN (NEWTOWNABBEY)
SEE UNDER Jordanstown

NEWTOWNARDS BRANCH LIBRARY
Queen's Hall, Regent Street
NEWTOWNARDS, BT23 4AB

TELEPHONE: 01247–814732; FAX: 01247–810265

HOURS:
MON–WED: 10:00 am–8:00 pm;
FRI: 10:00 am–8:00 pm;
SAT: 10:00 am–1:00 pm, 2:00 pm–5:00 pm

ACCESS:
Visitors welcome, but identification required. Borrowing privileges for visitors may be restricted. Consult with Librarian. Entire collection of 20,000 volumes catalogued in machine readable form. Handicapped accessible. No library parking available, but public car park nearby.

CONTACT PERSON: Mrs. Joan Thompson, Branch Librarian; Mrs. April Mercer, District Librarian

SERVICES:
Computerized access to NEELB and SEELB catalogues; photocopying and microfiche reader.

SEE ALSO: SOUTH EASTERN EDUCATION AND LIBRARY BOARD, Ballynahinch

NEWTOWNSTEWART BRANCH LIBRARY
2 Main Street
NEWTOWNSTEWART, BT78 4AA

TELEPHONE: 016626–61245

HOURS:
TUE: 1:00 pm–8:00 pm;
TH–FRI: 10:00 am–1:00 pm, 2:00 pm–5:30 pm;
SAT: 10:00 am–1:00 pm

ACCESS:
Visitors welcome, but identification required. Borrowing privileges for visitors may be restricted. Consult with Librarian. Handicapped accessible from rear of building.

CONTACT PERSON: Post vacant.

SEE ALSO: WESTERN EDUCATION AND LIBRARY BOARD, Omagh

O

CENTRE FOR EMIGRATION STUDIES
Ulster–American Folk Park, Mellon Road,
Castletown
OMAGH, BT78 5QY

TELEPHONE: 01662–243292; FAX: 01662–242241
E–MAIL: uafp@iol.ie

HOURS:
MON–FRI: 9:30 am–4:30 pm

ACCESS:
Open to the general public at no charge. Handicapped
accessible. Collection is catalogued on cards. Non-
circulating collection. Advance notification is preferred.
Access to the the Centre's Emigration Database (see
below) is also possible by direct dial in from the Local
History Departments of the Education and Library
Boards in Armagh, Ballymena, Ballynahinch, Belfast,
Enniskillen, Omagh and Derry.

CONTACT PERSON: Ms. Christine McIvor, Principal
Librarian

DESCRIPTION:
The Library is primarily a reference centre for migration
studies. It supports the Folk Park's main activities by
providing reference resources for the study of the history
of both the United States and Ireland in the eighteenth
and nineteenth centuries and the links between the two.
Library contains some 6,000 volumes, 1340 maps, plus
modest holdings of journals, microfilm, and recordings.
Collection emphasizes agriculture, architecture, crafts
and industry, social customs, religion and history as they
relate to the special interests of the Park. Library's
Emigration Database (see below) is an important support
resource for these activities. The Centre offers a part-
time MSSc. course in Migration Studies in association
with the Outreach Department at the Queen's University,
Belfast. This programme was inaugurated in September
1996.

SPECIAL COLLECTIONS:
Emigration Database contains primary source documents
on all aspects of Irish emigration to North America,
including Canada, from the early 1700s to the 1900s.
The Database consists of ship passenger lists, emigrant
letters, family papers and diaries of emigrants, shipping

advertisements, newspaper reports, death and marriage records of former emigrants, births of children of Irish parentage, government reports and statistics of Irish emigration to America and illustrated material showing ship types, ports, routes, and maps, shipboard conditions and the cost of the voyage to America. This is an ongoing project with documents being added on a regular basis.

PUBLICATIONS:
The Centre is the publications imprint of the Ulster-American Folk Park. A list of publications is available. The Park publishes various monographs and studies related to its mission, e.g., *The Mellon House; The Ulster-American Folk Park.* It also publishes a newsletter, *Conestoga.* The Centre also publishes proceedings of conferences held there, e.g., *"The Hungry Stream:" Essays on Migration and the Famine,* a selection of papers presented at the Folk Park's 1995 conference to commemorate the sesquicentenary of the outbreak of the Great Famine in 1845.

SERVICES:
Photocopying; leaflets; reference services; ample parking.

SEE ALSO: ULSTER-AMERICAN FOLK PARK, Omagh

OMAGH BRANCH LIBRARY
1 Spillars Place
OMAGH, BT78 1HL

TELEPHONE: 01662–244821; FAX: 01662–246772

HOURS:
MON, WED, FRI: 9:15 am–5:30 pm;
TUE, TH: 9:15 am–8:00 pm;
SAT: 9:15 am–1:00 pm, 2:00 pm–5:00 pm

ACCESS:
Visitors welcome, but identification required. Borrowing privileges for visitors may be restricted. Consult with Librarian. Handicapped accessible.

CONTACT PERSON: Ms. G. McSourley, Senior Librarian; for Irish and Local Studies, Senior Librarian (Local Studies)

DESCRIPTION:
Attractive, new facility with a strong Irish and Local Studies Department.

SPECIAL COLLECTIONS:
Irish and local studies collection houses some 5,000
volumes, plus strong holdings of maps, microforms,
journals and newspapers. Special focus on Co. Tyrone.
Includes microfilm copy of 1901 census for Co. Tyrone.

SERVICES:
Photocopying; microfilm reader/printer; lists; leaflets.

SEE ALSO: WESTERN EDUCATION AND LIBRARY BOARD,
Omagh

ULSTER–AMERICAN FOLK PARK
Mellon Road, Castletown
OMAGH, BT78 5QY

TELEPHONE: 01662–243292; FAX: 01662–242241
E–MAIL: uafp@iol.ie

HOURS:
EASTER–SEPTEMBER: MON–SAT: 11:00 am–6:30 pm;
SUN. AND HOLIDAYS: 11:30 am–7:00 pm;
OCTOBER–EASTER: MON–FRI: 10:30 am–5:00 pm

ACCESS:
Open to general public. Admission charged. Current
fees: Adult = £3.50; Child = £1.70 (under age 5 free);
group and family rates available.

CONTACT PERSON: John A. Walsh, Head of Museum
Services.

DESCRIPTION:
Large and sophisticated outdoor museum devoted to
telling the story of emigration to the New World in the
eighteenth and nineteenth centuries. Restored and
replicated structures, including a full-scale emigrant
ship, offer the visitor an opportunity to visit Ireland in
pre-twentieth century times, board an emigrant ship and
emerge in the New World. Exhibits trace the history of
the times, with special attention to agriculture, crafts,
transportation and society. A wonderful place to
entertain and educate children while adults visit the
Park's Centre for Emigration Studies.

SERVICES:
Exhibitions, symposia; residential centre; shops,
restaurant; conference facilities; bureau de change;
ample parking.

SEE ALSO:
CENTRE FOR EMIGRATION STUDIES, Omagh; Also ARMAGH COUNTY MUSEUM, Armagh; CAVAN COUNTY MUSEUM, Ballyjamesduff; NORTH DOWN HERITAGE CENTRE, Bangor; ULSTER MUSEUM, Belfast; ULSTER FOLK AND TRANSPORT MUSEUM, Cultra; TOWER MUSEUM, Derry; DOWN COUNTY MUSEUM; Downpatrick; ENNISKILLEN CASTLE, Enniskillen; DONEGAL COUNTY MUSEUM, Letterkenny; IRISH LINEN CENTRE AND LISBURN MUSEUM, Lisburn; and MONAGHAN COUNTY MUSEUM, Monaghan.

THE ULSTER HISTORY PARK
Cullion
OMAGH, COUNTY TYRONE

TELEPHONE: 016626–48188; FAX: 016626–48011

HOURS:
APRIL–SEPTEMBER: MON–SAT: 10:30 am–6:30 pm;
SUN: 11:30 am–7:00 pm;
OCTOBER–MARCH: MON–FRI: 10:30 am–5:00 pm;
PUBLIC HOLIDAYS: 10:30 am–7:00 pm.
Last admission 90 minutes before closing.

ACCESS:
Outdoor theme park open to the public. Admission charged. Current (1997) fees: Adults = £3.25; Child, Student, Senior, Registered Disabled = £1.95; Group and family rates available.

CONTACT PERSON: Mrs. Elizabeth Harkin, Education/ Promotions Officer

DESCRIPTION:
This 35-acre park traces the history of settlement in Ireland from stone-age hunters and gatherers who first settled in Ireland around 8,000 B.C. to the arrival of the 17th century Plantation settlers. Full-scale models of homes and monuments have been constructed. These range from the skin-covered hut of the earliest settlers to the stone-built fortified bawn and water powered corn mill of the Plantation period. A 'rath' or ringfort, is the most common field monument in Ireland, and the reconstruction in the Park gives an idea of what one of the 40,000 of these monuments might have looked like when it was inhabited by a farming family in the early Christian times, while a 'crannog,' an artificial island dwelling, was the home of the well-to-do of the same period. Ritual and ceremonial monuments in the park

O

include examples of megalithic tombs, a stone circle, and the stone church and round tower of an early Christian monastery. Special programs are often offered to add to the experience, e.g., volunteers wearing mediaeval costumes offering drinks made from herbs grown on site. The Park currently has a room for a library but no collection as yet.

SERVICES:
Indoor exhibition gallery; audio-visual programme; conference facilities; cafeteria; shop; picnic area; ample free parking.

SEE ALSO:
ULSTER FOLK AND TRANSPORT MUSEUM, Cultra; ULSTER-AMERICAN FOLK PARK, Omagh

WESTERN EDUCATION AND LIBRARY BOARD
Library Headquarters, 1 Spillars Place
OMAGH, BT78 1HL

TELEPHONE: 01662–244821

HOURS:
MON–FRI: 9:00 am–5:00 pm

ACCESS:
By appointment

CONTACT PERSON: Mr. R. Farrow, Chief Librarian

DESCRIPTION:
The administrative headquarters for the western library region, WELB oversees two divisional libraries (SOUTH WEST DIVISIONAL LIBRARY, Enniskillen, and NORTH WEST DIVISIONAL LIBRARY, Derry, and sixteen branch libraries (CASTLEDERG, CREGGAN, DERRY CENTRAL, DERRY SHANTALLOW, DERRY STRATHFOYLE, DERRY WATERSIDE, DUNGIVEN, ENNISKILLEN, FINTONA, IRVINESTOWN, LIMAVADY, LISNASKEA, NEWTOWNSTEWART, OMAGH, SION MILLS, AND STRABANE. In addition, WELB operates school, special service and mobile libraries.

CRAIGAVON DIVISIONAL LIBRARY
Headquarters, 113 Church Street
PORTADOWN, BT62 3DB

TELEPHONE: 01762–335247/335296; FAX: 01762–391759

HOURS:
MON–FRI: 9:00 am–5:00 pm

ACCESS:
By appointment
CONTACT PERSON: Mr. G. Burns

SEE ALSO: SOUTHERN EDUCATION AND LIBRARY BOARD, Armagh

THE INFORMATION SERVICE
113 Church Street
PORTADOWN, BT62 3DB

TELEPHONE: 01762–335247/335296

HOURS:
MON–FRI: 9.00 am–5.00 pm

ACCESS:
By appointment
CONTACT PERSON: Mrs. S. Young

SEE ALSO: SOUTHERN EDUCATION AND LIBRARY BOARD, Armagh

PORTADOWN BRANCH LIBRARY
25 Edward Street
PORTADOWN, BT62 3LX

TELEPHONE: 01762–332499

HOURS:
MON, WED: 10:00 am–8:00 pm;
TUE, TH, FRI: 10:00 am–5:30 pm;
SAT: 10:00 am–5:00 pm

ACCESS:
Visitors welcome, but identification required. Borrowing

privileges available to visitors. No handicapped access.

CONTACT PERSON: Miss A. D'Arcy

SEE ALSO: SOUTHERN EDUCATION AND LIBRARY BOARD,
Armagh

PORTAFERRY LIBRARY
47 High Street
PORTAFERRY, BT22 1QU

TELEPHONE: 012477–28194

HOURS:
MON, WED: 2:00 pm–8:00 pm;
FRI: 10:00 am–1:00 pm, 2:00 pm–5:00 pm;
SAT: 10:00 am–1:00 pm

ACCESS:
Visitors welcome, but identification required. Borrowing
privileges for visitors may be restricted. Consult with
Librarian.

CONTACT PERSON: Mrs. Geraldine McGrattan, Branch
Librarian

SEE ALSO: SOUTH EASTERN EDUCATION AND LIBRARY BOARD,
Ballynahinch

PORTGLENONE BRANCH LIBRARY
19 Townhill Road
PORTGLENONE, BT44 8AD

TELEPHONE: 01266–822228

HOURS:
TUE, FRI: 2:30 pm–5:00 pm, 5:30 pm–8:00 pm;
TH, SAT: 10:30 am–1:00 pm, 2:00 pm–5:00 pm

ACCESS:
Visitors welcome, but identification required. Borrowing
privileges for visitors may be restricted. Consult with
Librarian.

CONTACT PERSON: Mrs. C. Mulholland, Senior Library
Assistant in charge

SEE ALSO: NORTH EASTERN EDUCATION AND LIBRARY
BOARD, Ballymena

PORTRUSH BRANCH LIBRARY
Technical College, Dunluce Street
PORTRUSH, BT56 8DN

TELEPHONE: 01265–823752

HOURS:
MON, TH: 10:30 am–1:00 pm, 2:00 pm–5:30 pm;
TUE, FRI: 10:30 am–1:00 pm, 2:00 pm–5:00 pm, 5:30 pm–8:00 pm;
SAT: 10:30 am–1:00 pm, 2:00 pm–5:00 pm

ACCESS:
Visitors welcome, but identification required. Borrowing privileges for visitors may be restricted. Consult with Librarian.

CONTACT PERSON: Miss F. McCallum, Senior Library Assistant in charge

SEE ALSO: NORTH EASTERN EDUCATION AND LIBRARY BOARD, Ballymena

PORTSTEWART BRANCH LIBRARY
Town Hall, The Crescent
PORTSTEWART, BT55 7AB

TELEPHONE: 01265–832712

HOURS:
MON, WED–FRI: 10:00 am–1:00 pm, 2:00 pm–5:30 pm;
TUE: 10:00 am–1:00 pm, 2:00 pm–8:00 pm;
SAT: 10:00 am–1:00 pm, 2:00 pm–5:00 pm

ACCESS:
Visitors welcome, but identification required. Borrowing privileges for visitors may be restricted. Consult with Librarian.

CONTACT PERSON: Mrs. J. Davies, Senior Library Assistant in charge

SEE ALSO: NORTH EASTERN EDUCATION AND LIBRARY BOARD, Ballymena

FLIGHT OF THE EARLS HERITAGE CENTRE
SEE RATHMULLAN HERITAGE CENTRE, Rathmullan

RATHMULLAN HERITAGE CENTRE
Main Street
RATHMULLAN, COUNTY DONEGAL

TELEPHONE: 074–58229, 074–58131; FAX: 074–58115

HOURS:
MAY–SEPTEMBER: MON–SAT: 10:00 am–6:00 pm;
SUN: 2:00 pm–6:00 pm;
MARCH–MAY: MON–SAT: 8:30 am–4:30 pm

ACCESS:
Privately-funded heritage centre. Visitors welcome.
Admission charged. Current fees: Adults = £1.50;
Children and Seniors = 75p; Family = £4. Not currently
handicapped accessible.

CONTACT PERSON: Dessie McLaughlin, Project Manager

DESCRIPTION:
The centre features a display of the life and times of the
Earls Hugh O'Neill and Rory O'Donnell, two of
Ireland's most famous chieftains, through a variety of
mediums, including models, art works, literature, a
small scaled model of a plantation town and wax models
in 17th century dress. It was from Rathmullan in 1607
that the famous Flight of the Earls took place. O'Neill
and O'Donnell planned to sail to Spain to seek Spain's
support for their cause to liberate Ireland. They were
diverted, instead, to France and eventually to Rome,
where they both died, O'Donnell in 1609 and O'Neill in
1616. Their departure was followed by the Plantation of
Ulster. Though the Centre has no archives, it traces the
history of one of the most critical events in Irish history.

DONEGAL ANCESTRY
Old Meeting House, Back Lane
RAMELTON, COUNTY DONEGAL

TELEPHONE: 074–51266; FAX: SAME

HOURS:
MON–FRI: 9:00 am–4:30 pm

ACCESS:
Private and publicly-funded genealogical research centre open to the public. Visitors welcome, but appointment preferred. A fee schedule for research services is available on request. Fees vary depending on time involved and length of report required.

CONTACT PERSON: Joan Patton, Manager

DESCRIPTION:
Donegal Ancestry is one of seven designated centres in the nine counties of Ulster that participate in the Irish Genealogical Project (IGP). This project aims to create a comprehensive database of all genealogical sources that are known to exist, including church records of all denominations, civil records, land valuations, census records, gravestone inscriptions and various other local sources. The centre offers a genealogical research service for County Donegal. Indexing began in 1986. Recorded sources include birth, marriage and death registers for County Donegal from 1864 (excluding non-Roman Catholic marriage entries); Griffith's primary valuation for all parishes of Donegal; tithe applotment books for all parishes of Donegal; estate records for Murray-Stewart Estate, Fort Stewart Rent Books (1823-1830) and William Conolly's Ballyshannon Estate; 1901 Census returns; census substitutes, such as List of Freeholders (1760 and 1769), Spinning Wheel Premium Lists (1796), Hearth Money Rolls (1665), Protestant Householders, Extract from Pynnars Survey (1619), Muster Rolls (1630), Pender's Census of Ireland (1659), Civil Survey (1640), and Landowners in Ireland (1871-1876); graveyard inscriptions for 23 parishes; National School Records; and commercial directories.

SERVICES:
Genealogical research services provided for a fee. The Centre is located in the historic Old Meeting House, which dates back in part to the 1640s. Parking on site is limited, but street parking available. Signs pointing to Donegal Ancestry are currently non-existent, but there are plans to correct this. Be prepared to stop and ask directions. NOTE: Ramelton is sometimes spelled Rathmelton, but pronounced Ramelton.

SEE ALSO:
ARMAGH ANCESTRY, Armagh; ULSTER HISTORICAL

FOUNDATION, Belfast; COUNTY CAVAN GENEALOGICAL RESEARCH CENTRE, Cavan; THE GENEALOGY CENTRE, Derry; HERITAGE WORLD, Dungannon; MONAGHAN ANCESTRY, Monaghan. ALSO: GENERAL REGISTER OFFICE, Belfast; and PUBLIC RECORD OFFICE OF NORTHERN IRELAND, Belfast.

RAMELTON COMMUNITY BRANCH LIBRARY

SEE DONEGAL COUNTY LIBRARY ADMINISTRATIVE CENTRE, Letterkenny

RANDALSTOWN BRANCH LIBRARY

34 New Street
RANDALSTOWN, BT41 3AF

TELEPHONE: 01849–472725

HOURS:
TUE, FRI: 2:30 pm–5:30 pm, 6:00 pm–8:00 pm;
WED, TH: 10:30 am–1:00 pm, 2:00 pm–5:30 pm;
SAT: 10:30 am–1:00 pm, 2:00 pm–5:00 pm

ACCESS:
Visitors welcome, but identification required. Borrowing privileges for visitors may be restricted. Consult with Librarian.

CONTACT PERSON: Mrs. C. McGonigal, Senior Library Assistant in charge

SEE ALSO: NORTH EASTERN EDUCATION AND LIBRARY BOARD, Ballymena

RAPHOE BRANCH LIBRARY

SEE DONEGAL COUNTY LIBRARY ADMINISTRATIVE CENTRE, Letterkenny

RATHCOOLE BRANCH LIBRARY

2 Rosslea Way
RATHCOOLE, BT37 9BJ

TELEPHONE: 01232–851157

HOURS:
MON, FRI: 10:00 am–8:00 pm;
TUE, TH: 10:00 am–5:30 pm;
WED, SAT: 10:00 am–1:00 pm

ACCESS:
Visitors welcome, but identification required. Borrowing
privileges for visitors may be restricted. Consult with
Librarian.

CONTACT PERSON: Mrs. J. Stafford, Librarian in charge

SEE ALSO: NORTH EASTERN EDUCATION AND LIBRARY
BOARD, Ballymena

RATHFRILAND BRANCH LIBRARY
John Street
RATHFRILAND, BT34 5QH

TELEPHONE: 018206–30661

HOURS:
TUE: 2:00 pm–8:00 pm;
WED; 10:00 am–5:00 pm;
FRI: 10:00 am–5:00 pm;
SAT: 10:00 am–5:00 pm;
CLOSED MON, TH.

ACCESS:
Visitors welcome, but identification required. Borrowing
privileges for visitors may be restricted. Consult with
Librarian. Local computerized catalogue. Handicapped
accessible

CONTACT PERSON: Mrs. H. Henning

SPECIAL COLLECTIONS:
The library is also known as the "Bronte Library" and
contains a good collection of material on the sisters
Anne, Charlotte and Emily Bronte. The former
Drumballyroney Church and School House where their
father, Patrick Bronte, preached and taught is only a few
miles from the library, 8 miles from Banbridge, Co.
Down. It is now called the Bronte Homeland
Interpretative Centre. A pamphlet, entitled "The
Brontes" was produced by SELB in 1985.

SEE ALSO: SOUTHERN EDUCATION AND LIBRARY BOARD,
Armagh

RATHLIN BRANCH LIBRARY
(Temporarily closed)

RICHHILL BRANCH LIBRARY
Maynooth Road
RICHHILL, BT61 9PE

TELEPHONE: 01762–870639

HOURS:
TUE, FRI: 10:00 am–1:00 pm, 2:00 pm–5:30 pm;
WED: 2:00 pm–5:30 pm;
TH: 10:00 am–1:00 pm, 2:00 pm–8:00 pm;
SAT: 10:00 am–1:00 pm

ACCESS:
Visitors welcome, but identification required. Borrowing privileges for visitors may be restricted. Consult with Librarian.

CONTACT PERSON: Miss J. Brown

SEE ALSO: SOUTHERN EDUCATION AND LIBRARY BOARD, Armagh

SAINTFIELD LIBRARY
SEE UNDER Ballynahinch

SION MILLS BRANCH LIBRARY
Church Square
SION MILLS, BT78 9HA

TELEPHONE: 016626-58513

HOURS:
MON, FRI: 10:00 am–1:00 pm, 2:00 pm–5:30 pm;
TUE: 1:00 pm–8:00 pm;
SAT: 10:00 am–1:00 pm

ACCESS:
Visitors welcome, but identification required. Borrowing
privileges for visitors may be restricted. Consult with
Librarian.

CONTACT PERSON: Position open

SEE ALSO: WESTERN EDUCATION AND LIBRARY BOARD,
Omagh

STRABANE BRANCH LIBRARY
Butcher Street
STRABANE, BT82 8BJ

TELEPHONE: 01504–883686

HOURS:
MON, WED, FRI: 9:15 am–5:30 pm;
TUE, TH: 9:15 am–8:00 pm;
SAT: 9:15 am–1:00 pm

ACCESS:
Visitors welcome, but identification required. Borrowing
privileges for visitors may be restricted. Consult with
Librarian.

CONTACT PERSON: Mrs. A. Harron

SEE ALSO: WESTERN EDUCATION AND LIBRARY BOARD,
Omagh

STRATHFOYLE BRANCH LIBRARY
Claragh Crescent
STRATHFOYLE, BT47 7HQ

TELEPHONE: 01504–860385

HOURS:
MON–FRI.(CLOSED WED.): 10:00 am–12:30 pm, 1:30–
5:30 pm;
SAT: 9:15 am–1:00 pm

ACCESS:
Visitors welcome, but identification required. Borrowing
privileges for visitors may be restricted. Consult with
Librarian.

CONTACT PERSON: Mr. P. McLaughlin

SEE ALSO: WESTERN EDUCATION AND LIBRARY BOARD,
Omagh

TANDRAGEE BRANCH LIBRARY
Market Street
TANDRAGEE, BT62 2BW

TELEPHONE: 01762–840694

HOURS:
MON: 2:00 pm–8:00 pm;
TUE–FRI: 10:00 am–1:00 pm, 2:00 pm–5:30 pm;
SAT: 10:00 am–1:00 pm, 2:00 pm–5:00 pm

ACCESS:
Visitors welcome, but identification required. Borrowing
privileges for visitors may be restricted. Consult with
Librarian.

DESCRIPTION:
Opened in 1973 to serve a village population of about
2,800 people, and the surrounding rural area, the library
has a collection of some 12,000 volumes of general
interest, with a small local history collection.

CONTACT PERSON: Mrs. S. Anderson

SEE ALSO: SOUTHERN EDUCATION AND LIBRARY BOARD,
Armagh

TEMPLEPATRICK BRANCH LIBRARY
23 The Village
TEMPLEPATRICK, BT39 0AA

TELEPHONE: 01849–432953

HOURS:
TUE, FRI: 1:30 pm–5:00 pm, 5:30 pm–8:00 pm;
SAT: 10:00 am–1:00 pm

ACCESS:
Visitors welcome, but identification required. Borrowing
privileges for visitors may be restricted. Consult with
Librarian.

CONTACT PERSON: Mrs. G. Doyle, Senior Library
Assistant in charge

SEE ALSO: NORTH EASTERN EDUCATION AND LIBRARY
BOARD, Ballymena

U

ULSTER–AMERICAN FOLK PARK
SEE UNDER Omagh

ULSTER FOLK AND TRANSPORT MUSEUM
SEE UNDER Cultra

ULSTER HISTORICAL FOUNDATION
SEE UNDER Belfast

ULSTER HISTORY PARK
SEE UNDER Omagh

ULSTER MUSEUM
SEE UNDER Belfast

UNIVERSITY OF ULSTER AT BELFAST
SEE UNDER Belfast

UNIVERSITY OF ULSTER AT COLERAINE
SEE UNDER Coleraine

UNIVERSITY OF ULSTER AT JORDANSTOWN
SEE UNDER Jordanstown

UNIVERSITY OF ULSTER AT MAGEE
SEE UNDER Derry

VIRGINIA BRANCH LIBRARY
SEE CAVAN COUNTY COUNCIL BRANCH LIBRARIES, Cavan

W

WARINGSTOWN BRANCH LIBRARY
Village Hall, Main Street
WARINGSTOWN, BT66 7QH

TELEPHONE: 01762–881077

HOURS:
MON, TH: 2:00 pm–5:30 pm;
TUE: 2:00 pm–8:00 pm;
FRI: 10:00 am–1:00 pm, 2:00 pm–5:30 pm;
SAT: 10:00 am–1:00 pm

ACCESS:
Visitors welcome, but identification required. Borrowing
privileges for visitors may be restricted. Consult with
Librarian.

CONTACT PERSON: Mrs. C. L. Hamel

SEE ALSO: SOUTHERN EDUCATION AND LIBRARY BOARD,
Armagh

WHITEHEAD BRANCH LIBRARY
17B Edward Road
WHITEHEAD, BT38 9QB

TELEPHONE: 019603–53249

HOURS:
TUE, FRI: 10:00 am–1:00 pm, 2:00 pm–5:00 pm, 5:30
pm–8:00 pm;
WED: 10:00 am–1:00 pm, 2:00 pm–5:30 pm;
SAT: 10:00 am–1:00 pm, 2:00 pm–5:00 pm

ACCESS:
Visitors welcome, but identification required. Borrowing
privileges for visitors may be restricted. Consult with
Librarian.

CONTACT PERSON: Mrs. H. Lynagh, Senior Library
Assistant in charge

SEE ALSO: NORTH EASTERN EDUCATION AND LIBRARY
BOARD, Ballymena

APPENDIX

TITHE AND VALUATION RECORDS FOR ULSTER
c.1823–c.1930
Brian Trainor

Farmers of most agricultural land in Ireland were liable to pay to the rector of the established Church of Ireland a tithe or tax of one tenth of the yearly produce of the land and stocks. This tax was especially unpopular with Presbyterians and Roman Catholics. Agitation against the tax forced the Government to change the law and make the tithe charge a financial one (instead of crops etc.) and levied on the landlord rather than on the tenant. In order to determine the amount of money to be charged in lieu of tithe all agricultural land liable to tithe had to be surveyed and valued. This work was done by local surveyors and the detail given is variable; unfortunately there are no maps accompanying the survey showing the locations of farms. The surveys provide the names of lease-holding tenants in each townland and thus serve as a sort of a farm census for the whole country. The tithe surveys for parishes in Northern Ireland for the years 1823-38 are deposited in the Public Record Office of Northern Ireland and those for the Republic of Ireland are available in the National Archives, Dublin. In order to conserve the original documents only microfilm copies of these surveys are produced to the public.

The earliest full valuation of property in Ireland was carried out in the 1830s. This valuation was carried out in each townland and parish and the surveyor's manuscript field books of this 'townland valuation' for parishes in Northern Ireland are deposited in the Public Record Office of Northern Ireland (ref. VAL 1B) and those for the Republic are in the National Archives. No detail is given of buildings unless these were valued at £3.00 or more and this lower limit was raised to £5.00 in 1838 thus excluding most rural houses. Fortunately, most of Ulster was valued before the threshold was raised to £5.00. with the result that many buildings in the North around £2.00 valuation are included. In towns many houses were substantial enough to reach the valuation of £3.00 or £5.00

and in these cases detailed measurements of rooms and outbuildings are sometimes given as well as names of occupiers. For the town of Downpatrick the names of 330 occupiers are given in the field book for the parish of Down c.1838 (VAL 1B/378).

The National Archives, Dublin has another set of these field books for most parishes in Northern Ireland except for Co Tyrone. The National Archives, Dublin reference for the field book for the parish of Down is OL4.0459.

The first detailed valuation of <u>all</u> properties in Ireland was started in the province of Leinster during the Great Famine in 1848, and the valuation was completed in Northern Ireland 1858-64. The manuscript field books of this valuation for Northern Ireland are held in PRONI (ref. VAL 2B) and also the annual revisions recording changes in occupancy, consolidation of farms and the upheavals resulting from the Land Acts from the 1880s up to c.1930 (ref. VAL 12B).

Sir Richard Griffith, the great Commissioner of Valuation who was responsible for these massive surveys by central government arranged that a summary version of the valuation of 1848-64 for the whole country be made available in print. Some 200 volumes were published as official papers, one for each Poor Law Union or part. This printed valuation is popularly known as 'Griffith's Valuation'. It is doubtful if any country in the world has such ready access in printed form to records detailing the value and acreage of farms and buildings, with usually the names of landlords and the exact locations marked on official maps held in the Public Record Office of Northern Ireland and in the Valuation Office, Ely Place, Dublin. The tenement valuation records in the Republic have not yet been transferred to the National Archives.

The following list provides the exact references for tithe and valuation records for the parishes of Ulster that are held in PRONI and the National Archives. This will be of particular use to family and local historians.

PARISH	TITHES 1823–38 FIN 5A/	VALUATION 1830s VAL 1B/ FIELD BOOKS [OL4·]	TENEMENT VALUATION c.1861–2 VAL 2B/1	VALUATION REVISIONS c.1860–c.1930 VAL 12B/
Aghagallon	3	165A-B [·0069]	54	9/1A-E
Aghalee	4	166 [·0070]	58B	9/2 A-E
Ahoghill	10	15D, 176 179, [·0001], [·0059, ·0080], [·0082]	64 A-C	3/1 A-E, 3A-D, 4A, 5A-J, 9A-D, 14A-F, 18A-E, 19A-D
Antrim	13	16, [·0083]	5A-C, 51,	1/1A- F, 2A-C, 3A-C, 11A, 12A
		180	69	22A-E, 28A-E
Ardclinis	15	147A-B [·0050]	38	7/1A-E
Armoy	21	130, [·0032] 141, [·0044]	23A-B 37	2/1A-E 4/1A-D
Ballinderry	26	167, [·0071]	55A-B, 58B	9/3A-C
Ballintoy	27	131, [·0033]	24A-B	2/2A-E, 6A-D, 8/1A-E, 8A-E, 9/3A-E, 9A-E, 10A-F, 17A-E
Ballycastle (Ramoan)		280	2B, 1/28C	2/4A, 5A-C
Ballyclare (B'linny and B'nure)			7B	5A-B, 6A-B
Ballyclug	30	11, [·0002]	1	3/2A-E, 4A, 5A-V
Ballycor	24	[·0007/8]	6, 11	4A-E, 7/2A-D
Ballyeaston (B'cor & Rashee)	24			
Ballylinny	38 & 67	112, [·0014]	7A	1/4A-E, 7A-F
Ballymartin	39 & 67	113, [·0015] 124, [·0025]	11	1/14A-F, 29A-F
Ballymoney	40	142A-D 154 [·0045]	35A-F 50A	4/3A-G, 5A-E, 12A-E, 14A-F, 23A-F, 24A-D
Ballymena (Kirkinriola)			66A-F	3/5K-V
Ballynure	44	114, [·0016]	11, 12	1/4A-E, 7/3A-E
Ballyrashane	46	137, [·0039] 30/14A-D	30A* 6/1A-C	4/4 A, 5A-E,
Ballyscullion	47	181, [·0084]	72B	3/4A, 6A-E
Ballyscullion Grange of	Nil	182, [·0089]		3/4A, 6A-E

PARISH	TITHES 1823–38 FIN 5A/	VALUATION 1830s VAL 1B/ FIELD BOOKS [OL4·]	TENEMENT VALUATION c.1861–2 VAL 2B/1/	VALUATION REVISIONS c.1860–c.1930 VAL 12B/
Ballywillin	51	137, [·0040]	30A	4/4A; 6/1A-C, 2A-E
Belfast	36	see Shankill	18, 21A-D	43/
Billy	56	132, [·0034] 138, [·0041]	24B 25A-B 31	2/6A-D, 9A-E, 10A-F, 4/5A-E, 6A-C, 7A-E, 30/8A-D
Blaris	57	168, [·0072]	56A-B 3	8/9A-T, 10A-C, 11A, 12A-E, 20/6A-G, 16A-E
Broughshane (Racavan)			3C	3/7A-E
Bushmills (Billy)			26	4/6A-C; 30/8A-D
Camlin	63	169, [·0073]	52	1/16A-F
Carncastle	66	150, [·0055]	42	7/4A-E
Carnmoney	67	115A-B, [·0017]	13A-B	5/7A-G, 12A-K
Carrickfergus	70	187, [·0031]	22A-E,	7/5A-F, 6A-D, 7A-C
Connor	83	12, [·0003] 8A	2A-B, 18A-E	1/13A-E, 3/4A,
Craigs	See 10 (Ahoghill)	155 176 178 A-B	45 65A-B	3/3A-D, 4A, 13A-E, 14A-F, 19A-D 20A-D
Cranfield	85	183, [·0085]	70	1/15A-F
Crumlin (Camlin)			51	1/16A-F
Culfeightrin	87	133, [·0035]	27A-B 15A-D, 16A-D	2/8A-D, 11A-F,
Derryaghy	91B	125, [·0026] 170, [·0074]	19A-B 57	8/2A-G, 5A-E
Derrykeighan	93	134, [·0042] 139A-B	32	4/5A-E, 10A-E
Dervock (Derrykeighan)			33	4/10A-E
Doagh, Grange of	102	17A-B, [·0009]	7A	1/4A-E
Doagh, Village of		7B		
Donegore		18, [·0010]	8A-B	1/17A-E
Drumbeg	117	126	20	8/15A-J, 20/3A-E
Drummaul (Randalstown)	124	184, [·0086]	71A-D	1/10B-E, 3/9A-D, 11A-D,

PARISH	TITHES 1823–38 FIN 5A/	VALUATION 1830s VAL 1B/ FIELD BOOKS [OL4·]	TENEMENT VALUATION c.1861–2 VAL 2B/1	VALUATION REVISIONS c.1860–c.1930 VAL 12B/
				22A-F; 23A, 24A, 27A-E, 28A-E
Drumtullagh, Grange of	Nil	25B	2/9A-C	2/9A-E
Dunaghy	128	156, [·0060]	46A-B	3/4A, 8A-D, 22A-D
Dundermot, Grange of	130	157, [·0062]	46B	3/4A, 12A-D
Duneane	132	185, [·0087]	71D 72A-B	3/4A, 25A-E 10A-E, 15A-F
Dunluce	134	140	34A-B	4/4A, 5A-E, 21A-C, 6/1A-C, 2A-E
Finvoy	142	158A-C [·0061]	47A-B	4/11A-E, 12A-E, 25A-E
Glenavy	147*	171, [·0075]	58A-B	8/4A-D; 9/3A-E
Glenarm (Tickmacrevan)			41B	7/9A-H, 10A-E
Glenwhirry	Nil	13, [·0004]	3A	3/4A, 17A-D
Glynn	149	116	14	7/11A-D
Gracehill (Ahoghill)			64D	
Inispollan, Grange of	Nil	[·0051]	39	2/14A-E,
Inver	158	117, [·0019]	14	7/14A-G, 15B-M
Island Magee	159	118, [·0020]	15	7/12A-G
Kilbride	162	19, [·0011]	8B	1/4A-E, 20A-F
Killagan	172	144, 159, [·0047]	48	4/15A-F
Killdollagh	169	[·0063, ·0046]		30/14A-D
Killead	174	164A-C [·0068]	53A-C	1/8A-F, 9A-F, 19A-E, 26A-E
Killyglen, Grange of	181	151, [·0056]	44A	7/4A-E
Kilraghts	188	145, [·0048]	36	4/18A-E
Kilroot	190	119, [·0021]	16	7/18A-E
Kilwaughter	192	152A-B, [·0057]	43	7/13A-F
Kirkinriola	194	177, 66B-F, [·0081]	66A**	3/4A, 5A-V, 14A-F, 19A-D

* See also FIN 5A/63 and 269

** includes mill book

PARISH	TITHES 1823–38 FIN 5A/	VALUATION 1830s VAL 1B/ FIELD BOOKS [OL4·]	TENEMENT VALUATION c.1861–2 VAL 2B/1/	VALUATION REVISIONS c.1860–c.1930 VAL 12B/
Lambeg	196	127, [·0028] 172, [·0076]	59	8/7A-D, 9L 20/10A-F
Larne	197	153, [·0058]	44A-C	7/14A-G, 15A-M, 16A
Layd	198	148A-D [·0053]	40A-B 19A-F	2/7A-E, 14A-F,
Layd, Grange of	Nil	[·0052]	39	2/14A-D
Lisburn	(See Blaris)		61A-D	
Loughguile	208	146A-D, [·0049] 160, [·0064]	37 & 48	4/1A-D, 2A-D, 8A-E, 9A-D, 15A-F
Magheragall	217	174, [·0077]	55B 62A-B	8/6A-F, 13A-E
Magheramesk	221	175, [·0078]	62B	8/14A-D
Mallusk Grange of	259	[·0067]		
Muckamore Grange of	Nil	163	52	1/1A-F, 2A-C, 3A-C,
Newtown Crommelin	228	161, [·0065]	49, 21A	3/22A-D
Nilteen Grange of	110	9, [·0012]	17A-E	
Portglenone	232	178A-B	67A-C	3/1A-E, 4A, 20A-D, 23A-E
Portrush (Ballywillin)			30B	4/22A-D
Racavan	250	14A-B, [·0005]	3A-B	3/4A, 7A-E, 24A-D
Raloo	234	120, [·0022]	17A-B	7/17A-E
Ramoan (Ballycastle)	235	135, [·0037]	28A-B	2/3A-G, 16A-D, 17A-E
Randalstown (Drummaul)			71E	23A, 24A
Rasharkin	236	162, [·0066]	50A-B	3/4A, 13A-E, 15A-D, 4/16A-F, 17A-E
Rashee	24	111, [·0013]	10	1/25A-F
Rathlin Is.	238	136, [·0038]	29	17A-E, 18A-D
Shankill	36 247	121A-B, [·0023] 128 A-B, [·0028]	18 21A-D	5/3A-F, 4A-D, 5A-E, 6A-E, 8A-F
Shilvodan Grange of	83	186, [·0088]	73	28A-E
Skerry	250	15A-C, [·0006]	4A-C	3/7A-E, 16A-D, 21A-D

PARISH	TITHES 1823–38 FIN 5A/	VALUATION 1830s VAL 1B/ FIELD BOOKS [OL4·]	TENEMENT VALUATION c.1861–2 VAL 2B/1	VALUATION REVISIONS c.1860–c.1930 VAL 12B/
Stranocum (See Ballymoney)			33	
Templecorran	257	122	16	7/18A-F
Templepatrick	259	123A-B, [-0024] 129A-B, [-0030]	7B, 10, 11, 18, 21C	1/14A-F, 29A-F
Tickmacrevan (Glenarm)	263	149, [-0054]	41A,	7/9A-H, 10A-E
Tullyrusk	269 & 147	173A-B	63	8/16A-D
Whitehead				7/19A

PARISH	TITHES 1823–38 FIN 5A/	VALUATION 1830s VAL 1B/ FIELD BOOKS [OL4·]	TENEMENT VALUATION c.1864 VAL 2B/2/	VALUATION REVISIONS c.1860–c.1930 VAL 12B/
Acton			32D	
Armagh	20	21A & B, 224 234, [·0090] [·0110]	1A-G, 22	10/4A-H, 5A-C, 6A-C, 7A-C, 8A-C, 9A-E, 25A-E
Ballymore	41	214, 248 [·0120]	32A-C, 32E	11/1A-C, 11/5A-G, 15/23A-D, 15/24A-D
Ballymyre	42	239, [·0102]	13	15/2A-D
Blackwatertown		249	2B	
Camlough		178		
Charlemont (Loughgall)		249	2B	
Clonfeacle	79	22, 225A & B 234, [·0111]	2A, 23	10/12A-F, 23A-E, 30A-E, 38A-D,
Creggan	86	240A & B [·0103]	14A-G	12/2A-E, 3A-4E, 5A-E, 6A-E, 7A-D, 13/1A-F
Crossmaglen (Creggan)			14G	
Derrynoose	95	23, 235, 248 [·0091, ·0131]	3A-C, 40	10/11A-E, 17A-E, 19A-D, 26A-C, 28A, 39A-E
Drumcree	119	226A & B, 234, [·0112]	24A-H	14/2A-C, 6A-C, 12A-13B, 14A
Eglish	136	24, 236, 248 [·0092, ·0132]	4, 41	10/10A-D, 22A-E
Forkhill	143	215, 247, 248 [·0121, ·0126]	32E, 35A-C	12/5A-C, 15/13A-B, 18A-D, 24A-C
Grange	150	25, 227, 234 [·0093, ·0113]	5, 25	10/23A-E, 25A-E, 31A-E, 33A-E
Jonesborough	160	243, 248 [·0127]	36	15/15A-C
Keady	161	26A-D, 237 248-9, [·0094] [·0133]	6A-D, 3B-C, 42	10/3A-B, 17A-E, 19A-D, 26A-C, 27A-C, 28A-B
Kilclooney	225	210A & B 216, 248, 249 [·0098, ·0122]	9A-C	10/13A-D, 29A-D, 34A-E
Kildarton	20 etc			10/24A-D, 25A-E, 29A-C
Killevy	178	217, 244A & B 248, [·0123] [·0128]	32E, 34C, 37A-J	12B, 15/1A-D, 1F, 1H, 3A-E, 6A-J, 15A-C, 17A-C, 18A-D, 22A-24C

PARISH	TITHES 1823–38 FIN 5A/	VALUATION 1830s VAL 1B/ FIELD BOOKS [OL4·]	TENEMENT VALUATION c.1864 VAL 2B/2/	VALUATION REVISIONS c.1860–c.1930 VAL 12B/
Killylea (Tynan)		249		
Killyman	183	228, 234, [·0114]	27	10/30A-C
Kilmore	186	218, 248 229A & B [·0115, ·0124]	26A-D, 33	10/25A-E, 11/4A-F, 31A-E, 33A-E, 37A-F
Lisnadill	202	27, 211, 241 [·0095, ·0099] [·0104]	8A, 10A-B 12B, 15	10/3A-D, 9A-E, 11A-E, 29A-D, 32A-E
Loughgall	206	28, 230, 234 249, [·0096]	7, 28A-C	10/2A-E, 10/25A-E, 31A-E, 33A-E, 38A-D
Loughgilly	207	212, 219 245A & B, 248 [·0100, ·0125]	11, 29, 34A-C, 38A -B	10/34A-C, 11/3A-D, 15/3A-E, 19A-D, 23A-D, 24A-D
Lurgan (Shankill)			20C-G	14/9A-H
Magheralin	219	220, 234, [·0106]	17	14/5A-C
Markethill (Mullaghbrack)			12C	
Middletown (Tynan)				43D
Montiaghs	223	221, 234 [·0107]	18	14/11A-C
Mountnorris				32D
Mullaghbrack	225	213, 231, 234 [·0101, ·0117]	12A-B, 29	10/24A-D, 34A-E, 11/3A-E
Newry	226	232, 234, 246A-E, 248 [·0118, ·0130]	39A-C	10/33A-D, 15/1A-H 22/16A-C, 17A-C, 18A-D
Newtownhamilton	229	242A & B [·0105]	16A-D	12/1A-D, 5A-E, 6A-E, 8A-E
Poyntzpass				32D
Portadown (Drumcree etc)			24E-H	14/13A-N
Richhill (Kilmore)			26E	
Seagoe	245	222, 234, [·0108]	19A-D	14/3A-C, 4A-C, 7A-C
Shankill	248	223A & B 234, [·0109]	20A-G	14/5A-C, 9H
Tandragee (Ballymore)			11	11/5A-G
Tartaraghan	255	233A & B 234, [·0119]	21A-C	10/2A-C, 30A-C, 14/15A-D
Tynan	270	29A & B 238, 248 [·0097, ·0134]	8A, B 43A-D	10/11A-E, 17A-E, 22A-E, 35A-E, 39A-E

PARISH	TITHES 1823–38 FIN 5A/	VALUATION 1830s VAL 1B/ FIELD BOOKS [OL4·]	TENEMENT VALUATION c.1861–2 VAL 2B/3	VALUATION REVISIONS c.1862–c.1930 VAL 12B/
Aghaderg	1	337, 351 [·0419]	42, 55B-D	16/14A-D, 18A-E, 22A-D
Annaclone	11	352 [·0438, ·0439]	56	16/1A-F
Annahilt	12	338A & B 383, [·0445]	35	20/1A-E
Ardglass	16	368, 311B [·0451]	70A-B	18/1A-F, 27A
Ardkeen	17	35, [·0388]	7A-B, 23, 27	28/2A-F, 23/19A-F
Ardquin	18	36, [·0389]	8	18/2A-F
Ballee	23	369, 311B, [·0452]	71	18/1A-F, 22A-E
Ballyculter	32	370, 311B [·0453]	72	18/11A-E, 22A-E, 25A-F
Ballyhalbert (St Andrew's)	33	[·0312, ·0395]	7B, 9	23/1A-4F, 19A-F
Ballykinler	35	376A & B 311B	76	18/5A-F
Ballynahinch			28B	
Ballyphillip Slanes & Witter (Portaferry)	45 & 49	37, [·0390]	10	18/20A-F, 23/27A-D
Ballytrustan	45 & 49	38, [·0391]	11	18/20A-D, 23/27A-D
Ballywalter	50	39, [·0392]	9	23/6A-F
Banbridge (Seapatrick)			64B, C	16/7A-C, 8B-D
Bangor	54	31, 315 [·0384, ·0398]	1A-C, 7B	23/7A-K, 8A
Blaris	57	324, 339 [·0406, ·0420],	24A, 43	9A-S, 20/6A-D, 16A-G
Bright	62	377, 311B [·0458]	77	18/15A-E
Castleboy	exempt	310, [·0393]	12	18/2A-F
Castlewellan (Kilmegan)			63B	18/4G
Clonallan	75	353, [·0440]	57A-C, 60A	22/5A-D, 23A-G, 25A-C
Clonduff	77	354, [·0432]	49A-C	22/6A-D, 10A-D, 12A-D, 20A-B, 20D, 20F-H
Clough			66D	18/5A-E
Comber	82	316A-C [·0407]	2, 16A & B 25A	18/5A-E, 11A-F, 20A-E, 20/11A-E, 23/3A-F

PARISH	TITHES 1823–38 FIN 5A/	VALUATION 1830s VAL 1B/ FIELD BOOKS [OL4·]	TENEMENT VALUATION c.1861–2 VAL 2B/3	VALUATION REVISIONS c.1862–c.1930 VAL 12B/
Crossgar			28B	16/9A-E, 18/6A-F, 27A
(See Kilmore)				
Donaghadee	104	32, [·0385]	3A-C	23/10A-C, 13A-E 15A-B
Donaghcloney	105	340, [·0423]	44A-B 46C	21/4A-F, 9A-F
Donaghmore	108	355, [·0441]	58A-B	22/9A-E, 11A-E
Down	111	378, [·0459]	78A-D	18/7A-K, 12A-E, 26A-E
Dromara & Magherahamlet	112	341, 356 384, [·0421], [·0433, ·0446]	36, 37, 50A-B	16/2A-E, 9A-E, 20/9A-D
Dromore	113	342, [·0422]	38A-F	16/10A-F, 21A-E, 23A-E, 20/2A-D
Drumballyroney	116	357A & B	59A-C	16/4A-E, 24A-E, 22/20A-B, 20D, 20F-H
Drumbeg	117	326, [·0408]	25B-C	20/3A-E, 10B-E
Drumbo	118	327, [·0409]	25A-C	20/3A-E, 7A-F, 11A-E
Drumgath	120	358 & A B	59C	22/10A-D, 20A, 20C, 20E-H
Drumgooland	122	359, [·0434]	51A-D	16/5A-F, 15A-D, 20A-E
Dundonald	131	317, [·0399]	17	17/8A-G, 23/5A-F
Dundrum			79	18/9A-E, 27A
Dunsfort	135	371, 311B [·0454, ·2360]	73	18/11A-11E
Garvaghy	146	343, 360 [·0424, ·0435]	39, 52	16/3A-E, 12A-E
Gilford			48E-F	16/13A-B
(See Tullylish)				
Grey Abbey	151	33, [·0386]	4	23/16A-F, 21A-E
Groomsport			5	
Hillsborough	152	344A & B	45A-C	20/5A-D, 14A-E
Holywood	exempt	318	18A-D	10A-G, 11A-E, 17/2A-J, 10A-D, 43L/1-2, 43N/1-2
Inch	154	372, [·0456]	74	18/13A-D
Inishargy	155	311A & B [·0394]	13	23/4A-F, 19A-F
Kilbroney	163	361, [·0442]	61A-B 65A	19/15A-E, 21A-F

PARISH	TITHES 1823–38 FIN 5A/	VALUATION 1830s VAL 1B/ FIELD BOOKS [OL4·]	TENEMENT VALUATION c.1861–2 VAL 2B/3	VALUATION REVISIONS c.1862–c.1930 VAL 12B/
Kilclief	164	373, 379 311B,[·0460]	70A	18/25A-F
Kilcoo	166	362 [·0436]	53A-B 62	19/7A-F, 11A-E
Kilkeel	171	390A & B [·0464]	81A-H	19/4A-E, 13A-E, 14A-J, 18A-E, 19A-F
Killaney	Nil	328, [·0410]	26	20/15A-D
Killinchy	179	319, 329, 335 [·0400, ·0411], [·0417]	19, 23, 27, 33	18/14A-E, 19A-E 23/3A-F, 18A-E, 28A-E
Killyleagh	182	331, 336 [·0412, ·0418]	34A-C 80B	18/6A-F, 16A-F 18/15A-E, 27A
Killough				
Kilmegan	184	363A & B 380, 311B 385,[·0447, ·0461]	63A, 66B-C 79	18/4A-G, 9A-E, 24A-E
Kilmood	185	320, [·0401]	20	23/18A-E
Kilmore	187	330, 386 [·0413, ·0448]	28A, 66A 68	18/6A-F, 18A-E, 19A-E, 23A-D
Kircubbin			5	
Knockbreda	195	321, 332 [·0402, ·0414]	18D, 21, 29	17/3A-B, 6A-H 20/7A-D
Knockbreda (Belfast Co. Borough)			43A/5-10, 15-23, 43K/1	43A/28-34, 38-39
Knockbreda (Ballymacarrett ED)			43A/28-34, 38-39	43A/28-34, 38-39
Lambeg	196	333, [·0415]	30	20/10A-F
Lisburn (See Blaris)			24B	
Loughbrickland			55A	
Loughinisland	209	387, [·0449]	66A-C	18/5A-F, 23A-D, 24A-E
Maghera	211	364, [·0437]	54	19/17A-F
Magheradrool	215	388A & B [·0450]	67A-B 68	18/3A-G, 10A-E 20/13A-E
Magherahamlet	112		68	18/10A-E, 20/9A-D
Magheralin	219	346, [·0425]	46A-C, 47C	21/1A-E, 6A-F, 7A-E
Magherally	220	345, [·0426]	40	16/19A-E
Moira	222	347, [·0427]	47A-C	21/7A-E
Newcastle (see Kilmegan)			53A	19/20A-D
Newry	Nil	365, 389 [·0465]	69A-K	16/3A-E, 22/7A-F, 14A-L, 16A-C, 17A-C, 19A-F

PARISH	TITHES 1823–38 FIN 5A/	VALUATION 1830s VAL 1B/ FIELD BOOKS [OL4·]	TENEMENT VALUATION c.1861–2 VAL 2B/3	VALUATION REVISIONS c.1862–c.1930 VAL 12B/
Newtownards	227	34, 322 [·0387, ·0403]	6A-D, 22A-B	23/21A-E, 22A-E, 23A-C, 24A-F, 25A-N
Newtownbreda (See Knockbreda)			31	
Portaferry (See Ballyphilip)			14	18/20A-F, 27A, 23/26A
Rathfriland (See Drumballyroney)			60B-C	22/21A-B, 22A-B
Rostrevor (See Rostrevor)			61C	
Rathmullan	239	374, 381, 311B, [·0395]	72, 80A	18/11A-E, 15A-E, 26A-E
St Andrews (See Ballyhalbert)	241	312, [·0462]		
Saintfield	242	334,	32A-C	18/19A-E, 20/18A-E
Saul	244	375, 311B [·0416, ·0457]	75	18/7A-K, 22A-E
Seaforde			66D	
Seapatrick	246	348A & B, 366, [·0428/9]	41, 64A 44A	16/6A-H, 8A-D, 19A-E
Shankill		349, [·0430]	46A, 47B	21/5A-D
Slanes	45	313, [·0396]	15	23/27A-D
Strangford			14	
Tullylish	266	350, [·0431]	44B, 48A-D	16/25A-H, 21/4A-F, 8A-F
Tullynakill	267	323, [·0404/5]	23	23/28A-E
Tyrella	271	382, 311B [·0463]	80A	18/26A-E, 27A
Waringstown (See Donaghcloney)			44C	
Warrenpoint	75	367, [·0443/4]	65A-B	23A-G, 25A-C
Witter	45	314, [·0397]		

PARISH	TITHES 1823–38 FIN 5A/	VALUATION 1830s VAL 1B/ FIELD BOOKS [OL4·]	TENEMENT VALUATION c.1861–2 VAL 2B/4	VALUATION REVISIONS c.1860–c.1930 VAL 12B/
Aghalurcher	6	428A-B, [·0502-4]	19A-E	28/5A-D, 6A-D, 7A-E, 10A-E, 11A-E, 19A-E, 20A-E, 21A-E, 22A-F, 23A-F, 24A-E
	also D998/22/1			
Aghavea	8	429, [·0505-7]	20A-C	28/6A-E, 11A-E, 13A-E, 19A-E, 22A-F
Belleek	55	415A-B, [·0490]	10	24/1A-E, 2A-E, 7A-E
Boho	60	41, 422, [·0466] [·0496]	1 & 15	24/6A-E, 26/1A-E, 22A-E, 37A-D
Cleenish	72	42, 432, 430A & B, 432, [·0467-9] [·0497, ·0508-9] [·0511]	1, 2A-D 7E 21	24/6A-E; 26/7A-E, 10A-E, 19A-D, 20A-E, 23A-E, 24A-F, 30A-F, 31A-E, 32A-E, 37A-E
		430A-B		
Clones*	MIC 442/10	46, [·0474]	5A-D 6	25/1A-D, 2A-E, 3A- E, 5A-E, 7A-E, 8A-D, 10A-E
Currin*	MIC 442/10	47A-D, 49 [·0475]	6	
Derrybrusk	92	431, 433 [·0510, ·0512]	22	26/4A-E, 26A-E, 28/5A-E
Derryvullen	96	419 [·0491] [·0498] 434 [·0513]	11A-B 21, 22, 23A-C	26/2A-E, 3A-F, 5A-F,, 10A-E, 17A-K, 31A-E 27/9A-E, 11A-E, 13A-E, 15A-E,
Devenish	101	424 A-D [·0498]	16A-D	24/4A-E, 8A-E, 26/12A-F, 16A-E, 17A-K, 33A-E, 35A- E, 36A-E, 37A-E
Drumkeeran	123	416 A-B [·0492, ·3819]	12A-C	27/3A-E, 4A-E, 5A- E, 6A-E, 7A-F, 8A-E, 16A-E
Drummully Ederny	125	410A-C [·0476-9]	6, 7B 13D	25/2A-E, 4A-E
Enniskillen	137	425A-B 435A-B [·0499, ·0514]	20C, 23A & B 24A-H	26/3A-F, 4A-E, 5A-F, 6A-F, 17A-K, 18A-H, 25A-E,

PARISH	TITHES 1823–38 FIN 5A/	VALUATION 1830s VAL 1B/ FIELD BOOKS [OL4·]	TENEMENT VALUATION c.1861–2 VAL 2B/4	VALUATION REVISIONS c.1860–c.1930 VAL 12B/
		[·3820/1]		28/11A-E, 31A-E, 38A-F
Galloon	145	48, 411, 412 [·0478-81]	5B, 7A-E	25/3A-E, 4A-E, 6A-E, 7A-E, 8A-E, 9A-E, 28/3A-E, 7A-E, 8A, 14A-E
Inishmacsaint	156	426A-C [·0500]	17A-D	24/3A-E, 5A-E, 26/12A-F, 36A-E
Kesh			13D	
Killesher	177	43 [·0472, ·0482-6]	3A-C	26/9A-E, 11A-E, 13A-F, 19A-F, 27A-E
Kinawley	Nil	44, 413	4A-B 8A-E	26/9A-E, 11A-E, 28A-F, 29A-E, 28/1A-E, 2A-E, 12A-E, 15A-E, 16A-E, 17A, 25A-E
Lack (M'Culmoney)			13D	
Lisnaskea			27	
Magheracross	213	417, 436 [·0515]	25A-B	26/2A-E, 3A-F, 34A-F, 27/2A-E, 9A-F
Magheraculmoney	214	418 [·0493]	13A-D	27/7A-F, 10A-E, 12A-E, 14A-E, 15A-E
Newtownbutler (Galloon)			7F	
Pettigoe (T'carn)			12D	
Rosslea (Clones)			5E	
Rossory	240	45, 427A-B [·0473, ·0501]	18 & 24B	26/7A-E, 16A-E, 17A-K, 30A-F, 32A-E
Templecarn	MIC 442/9	421 A-B [·0494]	14	27/3A-E
Tempo			28	
Tomregan	MIC 442/2	414, [·0487-9]	9	28/2A-E
Trory	265	420 437A-B, [·0495] [·0516]	23C, 26	26/2A-E, 27/11A-E

* For border parishes, original records, were retained in Dublin and are now in the National Archives; microfilm copies MIC 442 in PRONI. Parishes include Clones, Currin, Templecarn and Tomregan

PARISH	TITHES 1823–38 FIN 5A/	VALUATION 1830s VAL 1B/ FIELD BOOK [OL4·]	TENEMENT VALUATION c.1858–9 VAL 2B/5	VALUATION REVISIONS c.1860–c.1930 VAL 12B/
Aghadowey	2	51	1A-C, 2	30/1A-E, 2A-E, 6A-F, 11A-E, 13A-F, 15A-E, 18A-E
Aghanloo	7	511, 520, [·1071]	17A-B	31/1A-E
Agivey	nil	52	2	30/2A-F, 34/2A-E
Arboe	14	522, [·1079] [·1079A]	25, 43A	34/26A-F
Artrea	22	523	26A-C, 43A	34/4A-E, 9A-G, 16A-E, 20A-F, 24A-F, 26A-F
Ballinderry	25	525, [·1081]	27, 43A	9/3A-C
Ballyaghran (Agherton)	28	539A & B 546A	10, 15A-B	30/4A-F, 17A-H
Ballymoney	40	540, 546A	11, 15B	4/3A-G
Ballynascreen	43	524, [·1082]	28A-C, 43A & C	34/5A-E, 8A-E, 12A-F, 25A-F
Ballyrashane	46	53, 546A & B [·1068]	12, 15B	30/14A-F
Ballyscullion	47	526, [·1083]	29A-B, 43B	34/6A-G, 9A-G
Ballywillin	51	541A-C, 546A	13, 15B	13A-G, 19A-E, 30/4A-F
Balteagh	52	513A & B 516, [·1072]	18	31/13A-G, 19A-E, 21A-E
Banagher	53	512A-E 548A & B [·1073, ·1095]	19, 44	31/11A-E, 12A-F, 21A-F
Bellaghy (See B'scullion)			29C	
Bovevagh	61	514A-C, 516 [·1074]	17B, 20A-B, 21C	31/6A-E, 14A-E, 23A-D
Camus (Macosquin)	64A			
Carrick[1]		515	17B, 24A	31/13A-G, 14A-E, 23A-E, 24A-E
Castledawson (B'scullion)			37H	
Clondermot (Glendermot)	76	549A-D	45A-D, 50	32/1A-G, 12A-F, 14A-F, 33/4A-C
Coleraine	81	53, 542A-D, 546A & C [·1069]	3B-F, 14, 15B	30/4A-G, 9A-D, 14A-D, 17A-H

1 This parish was created in 1846 from parts of Balteagh, Bovevagh and Tamlaght Finlagan

PARISH	TITHES 1823–38 FIN 5A/	VALUATION 1830s VAL 1B/ FIELD BOOKS [OL4·]	TENEMENT VALUATION c.1858–9 VAL 2B/5	VALUATION REVISIONS c.1860–c.1930 VAL 12B/
Cumber Lower	88	552, [·1096]	46, 50	32/1A-G, 4A-F, 13A-F
Cumber Upper	89	554, [·1097]	47A-B, 50	31/12A-F, 32/2A-F, 5A-F
Derry, Deanery of	91A			
Derryloran	94	527, [·1084]	30, 43A	34/19A-F
Desertlyn	98	528, [·1085]	31A-B, 43A & C	34/2A-E, 7A-E, 20A-F
Desertmartin	99	529, [·1086]	32A-B, 42 43A	34/2A-E, 7A-E, 11A-F, 14A-E
Desertoghill	100	54A-C	4A-B	29/1A-D, 30/6A-F, 12A-F, 19A-F
Drumachose	115	517A-F	17B, 22A-C	31/13A-G, 16A-E, 18A-G
Draperstown (Ballynascreen)			42	
Dunboe	129	55A & B	5A-C	30/3A-G, 5A-F, 10A-F
Dungiven	133	518A-C, [·1075]	21A-D	31/9A-F, 14A-E, 15A-F
Errigal	140	56	5C, 6A	30/12A-F, 13A-F, 31/12A-F, 13A-F, 18A-E, 19A-F
Faughanvale	141	550A & B [·1098]	48A-B, 50	31/3A-G, 10A-E, 32/6A-F, 12A-F
Fermoyle[2]	129		7	30/3A-E, 10A-E, 15A-E
Garvagh (Errigal)			6B	
Kilcronaghan	167	530, [·1087]	33A, 43A	34/8A-E, 14A-E, 28A-E
Kildollagh	169	543, 546A	15A-B	30/14A-F
Killelagh	196	532A & B [·1070]	34, 37A & D 43B	34/27A-E, 29A-E
Killowen	180	57	8	30/5A-F, 9A-D
Kilrea	189	58, 544, [·1088]	35, 43B	29/3A-F; 30/21A-21D
Learmont[3]	53	551	49A-B, 50	32/2A-F, 3A-F
Limavady (Drumachose)			22B-C	

2 This parish was created in 1843 out of Dunboe

3 This parish was created in 1831 from parts of Banagher and Cumber Upper and Lower

PARISH	TITHES 1823–38 FIN 5A/	VALUATION 1830s VAL 1B/ FIELD BOOK [OL4·]	TENEMENT VALUATION c.1858–9 VAL 2B/5	VALUATION REVISIONS c.1860–c.1930 VAL 12B/
Lissan	203	533A & B [·1089]	36A-B 43A & C	34/15A-F, 19A-F,
Londonderry (Templemore)			16C-H	
Macosquin	64A	59	5C, 9A-B	30/5A-F, 11A-F, 15A-E, 20A-F
Maghera	212	534A & B [·1090]	37A-G, 43B & C	34/8A-E, 11A-F, 13A-E, 17A-G, 23A-F, 27A-E, 29A-E
Magherafelt	216	535 [·1091]	38A-C, 43A	34/2A-E, 9A-G, 18A-F
Magilligan	252	519A-C, 520 [·1076]	17B, 23	31/1A-E, 3A-G, 4A-D, 5A-E
Moneymore			31B	
Swatragh			37G	
Tamlaght	251	536, [·1092]	39, 43A	34/26A-F
Tamlaghtard (Magilligan)	252			31/1A-E, 3A-G, 4A-F, 5A-E
Tamlaght Finlagan	253	521A-C [·1077]	24A-C	31/3A-G, 18A-G, 20A-G, 24A-E
Tamlaght O'Crilly	254	510, 537 545, 1093	40A-C, 43B	29/1A-D, 2A-D, 30/21A-D, 34/10A-F
Templemore	91A	547A-F, 553A-D [·1078]	16A-J	32/8A-G, 10A-G, 11A-ZD, 33/1A-B, 2A-F, 3A-C, 5A-C
Termoneeny	261	538A & B [·1094]	41, 43B-C	34/17A-G, 23A-F, 28A-E
Upperlands (Maghera)				34/30A

PARISH	TITHES 1823–38 FIN 5A/	VALUATION 1830s VAL 1B/	TENEMENT VALUATION c.1860 VAL 2B/6/	VALUATION REVISIONS c.1860–c.1930 VAL 12B/
Aghaloo	5	66B	6A-C	36/3A-D, 4A-B 38/3A-F, 8A-F, 21A-F
Aghalurcher	6	61A & B	1	36/11A-F, 14A-F
Arboe	14	618	18A-E 27	37/1A-F, 4A-G, 10A-F, 13A-G
Ardstraw	19	633A-F	35	35/5A-F, 8A-F, 17A-F
		637A-F	40A 47C	19A-F, 39/10A-E 41/27A-F, 42/1A-F, 2A, 7A-F, 12A-F, 17A-F, 27A-H
Artrea	22	619	19	37/4A-G, 21A-F
Ballinderry	25	620A & B	20	37/13A-G
Ballyclog	29	621A & B	21	37/1A-F
Beragh (Clogherny)		626A		
Bodoney Lower	58	643	45A-B	39/1A-E, 2A-E, 4A-D, 6A-E, 13A-D
Bodoney Upper	59	644 A & B	46 A-C	30/3A-E, 5A-F, 7A-G, 9A-G, 11A-G
Camus	64B & C	638 A-C	41	42/10A-G, 31A-M
Cappagh	65	626B 645A & B	28 47A-C	41/6A-F, 17A-F, 19A-F, 24A-F, 26A-F, 31A-F, 32A-G
Carnteel	68	68	6C, 7A-B	36/3A-D, 4A-B, 5A-B, 7A-F, 18A-F, 38/1A-F, 3A-F, 10A-F
Castlederg (Urney)		626A		35/1A, 6A-F
Coagh (Tamlaght)		66A		
Coalisland (D'henry)		66A		
Clogher	73	62A-K 647	2A-F	36/1A-F, 2A-F, 6A-F, 8A-F, 9A-F, 10A-F, 11A-F, 14A-F, 16A-G
Clogherney	74	627	29	41/4A-G, 6A-F, 14A-F, 35A-F, 39A-F

PARISH	TITHES 1823–38 FIN 5A/	VALUATION 1830s VAL 1B/	TENEMENT VALUATION c.1860 VAL 12B/6/	VALUATION REVISIONS c.1860–c.1930 VAL 12B/
Clonfeacle	79	610	9A-D	38/4A-F, 5A-F, 6A-F, 14A-F, 22A-F
Clonoe	80	69	10A-B	38/20A-F, 23A-F
Cookstown (Derryloran)		66A		
Cumber Upper		641		37/7A-C
Derryloran	84	622A & B	22A -B	37/5A-K, 7A-C, 11A-F, 15A-F, 21A-F
Desertcreat	97	623	24A-D	37/16A-F, 17A-F, 18A-F, 21A-F
Donacavey	103	63A & B, 628	2B, 3A-B 30	41/8A-F, 13A-E, 15A-F, 22A-F, 23A-F, 39A-F, 42A-E
Donaghedy	Nil	639A & B	42A-D	39/8A-E, 12A-E, 42/6A-G, 18A-G, 19A-G, 22A-F, 26A-G
Donaghenry	107	611	11A-B 18E	37/20A-G, 21A-F, 38/25A-F
Donaghmore	109A	612	12A-C	38/2A-F, 9A-F, 11A-F, 13A-F, 14A-F, 15A-F, 17A-N
Dromore	114	626A, 629	31A-B 33B	40/4A-F, 5A-F, 41/5-F, 16A-F, 25A-F, 43A-F
Drumglass	121	613	13	38/5A-F, 15A-F, 17A-N
Drumquin		626A		
Drumragh	126	630A & B	32A -B	41/6A-F, 10A-F, 29A-F, 34A-M, 36A-M, 39A-F
Dungannon Middle		617		38/17A-N
Errigal Keerogue	139	64A & B	4A-B	36/7A-F, 12A-F, 13A-F, 15A-F, 38/1A-F
Errigal Trough	MIC 442/10	65A-C	5	
Gortalowry		66A		
Irishtown		626A		
Kildress	170	624	24A 25A-C	37/2A-F, 9A-F, 14A-F, 15A-F

PARISH	TITHES 1823–38 FIN 5A/	VALUATION 1830s VAL 1B/	TENEMENT VALUATION c.1860 VAL 2B/6/	VALUATION REVISIONS c.1860–c.1930 VAL 12B/
Killeeshil	175	67	6C, 8	38/1A-F, 10A-F
Killyman	183	614	15A-C	38/5A-F, 16A-F
Kilskeery	191	631A & B	33A-B	40/1A-E, 2A-F, 4A-E 5A-F
Learmount*			42D	
Leckpatrick	201	640	43A-B	42/5A-G, 22A-F, 31A-M
Lissan	203	625	26	37/3A-F, 11A-F
Longfield East	204	633A-F	36	41/18A-F, 34A-F
Longfield West	205	633A-F	37A-B	35/4A-F, 9A-F, 11A-F, 21A-F
Loy		66A		
Omagh (Drumragh)				41/37A-G
Magheracross	213		33B	40/1A-E, 42/27A-H
Newtownstewart (Ardstraw)			40B	
Pomeroy	231	66A, 615	16A-D	37/16A-F, 38/2A-F, 13A-F
Stewartstown (Donaghenry)		66A		
Strabane (Camus & Urney)				42/31E-M
Tamlaght	251		27	37/4A-G
Tarmonrock		626A		
Termonamongan	260	633A-F	38A-C	35/10A-F, 13A-F, 14A-F, 16A-F, 20A-F
Termonmaguirk	262	632, 646	34A-C	41/2A-F, 7A-F, 12A-F, 28A-F, 35A-F, 40A-F
Trillick (Kilskeery)		626A		
Tullyniskan	268	616	17	38/25A-F
Urney	MIC 442/8B	633A-F 642	39, 44	35/6A-F, 13A-F, 16A-F, 42/1A-F, 20A-G, 31A-M

* one townland only in Co Tyrone parish created 1831 from parts of Banagher and Cumber Upper and Lower

PARISH	TITHES 1823–38 TAB 4/	FILM	VALUATION FIELD BOOKS 1830s OL4· HOUSE BOOKS [OL5·]	TENEMENT VALUATION c.1857 FICHE	1841–1851 CENSUS SEARCHES CEN S/4
Annagelliff	13	5	0224 [·0061] [·3787]	5 G 6	516-540
Annagh	16	5	0219 0220 0233 [·0060 ·0069/70]	5 A 6 5 F 2 7 C 8	470-482 782-803
Bailieborough	23	5A	0199 0206 [·3772/5, ·3798/9]	1 D 6 1 A 14	162-195
Ballintemple	26	5B	0212 [·0047]	4 B 8	284-341, 469
Ballyconnell			[·3800/01]		
Ballyjamesduff			[·3802]		
Ballymachugh	28	5B	0213 [·0048/9]	4 C 14	342-3
Belturbet (Annagh & Drumlane)			[·2387]		
Castlerahan	32	5B	2028A [·3764]	10 B 2	2-40
Castleterra	11	4	0225 [·0062/3]	6 A 6	541-581
Cavan			[·3803]		
Crosserlough	30	5B	0200, [·0038] 0214, [·0050/1] 0226, [·0064] 2029A, [·3764] [·3788]	6 C 3 4 D 10 4 F 10 10 C 11	41-86, 344-359 582-584
Denn	14	5	0201, [·0039] 0215, [·0052/3] 0227, [·3770] 2030A 2033A [·3789/90]	6 C 4 10 G 12 4 E 5 5 A 4 10 C 13	87-91, 360-365 412, 585-631
Drumgoon	19	5A	0207, [·0071] 0234	7 D 4 8 D 8	196-214, 632 804-824
Drumlane	6	4	0221	2 D 12 5 C 4	483-513
Drumlumman	27	5B	0216 [·0054/5]	4 E 9 9 D 4	366-440

PARISH	TITHES 1823–38 TAB 4/	FILM	VALUATION FIELD BOOKS 1830s OL4· HOUSE BOOKS [OL5·]	TENEMENT VALUATION c.1857 FICHE	1841–1851 CENSUS SEARCHES CEN S/4
Drumreilly			0238, [·0079] 0239	2 E 4	932-935
Drung	17	5	0235, [·0072/3]	7 F 3	825-857
Enniskeen	24	5A	0208, [·3776/8]	1 E 13	215-229
Kilbride	29	5B	0217, [·0056] [·3786]	4 E 9 10 F 14	441-449
Kildallan	7	4	0245	3 C 8 3 E 12	119-1134
Kildrumsherdan	18	5	0236, [·0074/6]	7 G 12	858-885
Killashandra	8	4	0246 [·3804]	3 D 10 3 F 2	1135-1210, 1212
Killinagh	1	3	0240, [·0080]	8 G 12	936-1007
Killinkere	31	5B	0202, [·0040] 0228, [·3766] 2034A, [·3791/2]	6 D 6 1 B 9 10 D 2	92-120, 635-645
Kilmore	12	4	0218, [·0057/8] 0229, [·0065] [·3793]	6 D 8 4 E 11	450-468, 646-675
Kinawley	3	4	0241, [·0081/2] 0242	2 E 6 9 B 6	1008-1032
Knockbride	21	5A	0209, [·3779/81] [·3813]	2 B 8 8 E 11	231-257
Larah	20	5A	0230, [·0066] 0237, [·0077/8] [·3794/6]	6 E 12 5 G 3 8 C 4	676-704 887-931
Lavey	15	5	0231, [·0067] [·3795/6]	6 F 7	705-757, 886
Loughan or Castlekeeran			[·0041] [·3767], [·3764]	9 G 10 10 D 3	121-123
Lurgan	33	5B	0203, [·0042] [·3768]	10 D 8	124-136
Moybolgue	25	5A	0210, [·3782]	1 G 13	258-262
Mullagh			0204 [·0043] 2031A, [·3771]	1 A 14 9 G 10 10 F 2	137-154
Munterconnaught			0205, [·0044] 2032A, [·3769]	10 F 4	155-161
Scrabby	9	4	0247 2037A	4 B 5 9 F 2	1211, 1213-1227
Shercock	22	5A	0211, [·0045] [·3784/5]	2 A 4	263-283

PARISH	TITHES 1823–38 TAB 4/	FILM	VALUATION FIELD BOOKS 1830s OL4· HOUSE BOOKS [OL5·]	TENEMENT VALUATION c.1857 FICHE	1841–1851 CENSUS SEARCHES CEN S/4
Swanlinbar			[·3808]		
Templeport	2	3	0243, [·0083/4]	2 F 8 9 B 7	1033-1105
Tomregan	5	4	0222, [·0059] 0244, [·0085/6]	3 B 10 2 D 13 5 E 13	514-515, 1106-118
Urney	10	4	0223, [·0068] 0232, [·3797]	5 E 14 6 G 10	758-781
Virginia			[·3806]		

The 1821 census is available in the National Archives for 16 parishes:

Annagelliff, Ballymachugh, Castlerahan, Castleterra, Crosserlough, Denn, Drumlumman, Drung, Kilbride, Kilmore, Kinawley, Larah, Lavey, Lurgan, Mullagh, Munterconnaught.

PARISH	TITHES 1823–38 TAB 7/	FILM	VALUATION FIELD BOOKS 1830s OL4· HOUSE BOOKS [OL5·]	TENEMENT VALUATION c.1857 FICHE	1841–1851 CENSUS SEARCHES CEN S/7
Aghanunshin	18	29	·0353, ·2316 [·0818]	9 A 12	671-680
Allsaints	29	30	·0365 [·0832]	9 G 6 11 A 2	1345-1357
Aughnish	16	29	·0354, ·2317 [·0819/20]	9 B 4 12 D 11	681-696
Ballintra (Drumhome)			[·2670]		
Ballyshannon (Kilbarron)			[·2670]		
Bundoran (Inishmacsaint)			[·2670] [·3810]		
Burt	25	30	·0346, ·2310/11 [·0816]	10 C 10	563-583
Carndonagh			·2306		
Clonca	1	27	·0340, ·2307	7 B 4	487-502
Clondahorky	10	28	·0355, ·2318 [·0821]	3 F 10	697-747
Clondavaddog	7	27	·0356, ·2319 [·0822]	13 B 4	748-808, 1667
Clonleigh	35	31	·0368, ·2329/30 [·0833]	14 C 5	1358-1384, 1387-8, 1930
Clonmany	2	27	·0341, ·2308	7 C 13	503-517 [T550/37 in PRONI]
Convoy	36	31	·0366, [·0834]	14 F 2	1528-1558
Conwal	17	29	·0357	9 D 1	809-882
			·0367	11 C 12	1559-1580
			2320/21, 2331	15 F 10	
Culdaff	4	27	·0342, 2309 [·0812/3]	7 E 10	518-526
Derry See Templemore					
Desertegny	20	29	·0347	8 E 8	584-595
Donagh	3	27	·0343	7 G 6	527-539
Donaghmore	39	31	·0369, 2332 [·0835]	13 E 8 14 G 12	1581-1621 1645
Donegal	49	32	·0378-79 [·2670]	2 G 6	1668-1715
Drumhome	49	32	·0380 [·0842]	1 A 12	1716-1799 1847
Fahan Lower	21	30	·0348	8 F 1	596-629
Fahan Upper	22	30	·0349, 2312	10 D 8	630-644

PARISH	TITHES 1823–38 TAB 7/	FILM	VALUATION FIELD BOOKS 1830s OL4· HOUSE BOOKS [OL5·]	TENEMENT VALUATION c.1857 FICHE	1841–1851 CENSUS SEARCHES CEN S/7
Gartan	14	29	·0358, 2322 [·0823]	4 A 7 9 B 6	883-905
Glencolumbkille	42	32	·0328, [·0802] ·2275, ·2284	4 G 8	1-51
Inch	24	30	·0350, 2313/14	10 E 5	645-653
Inishkeel	28	30	·0329, ·0336 ·2276, ·2285, ·2289/90, ·2300/02, ·2305 [·0803/04]	5 G 2 5 B 3	52-85 316-372
Inishmacsaint	52	32	·0381	1 E 8	1800-1808 1814-1819, 1824
Inver	46	32	·0330, [·0805/06] ·2277	2 B 2	86-187, 714
Kilbarron	51	32	·0379 ·0382	1 B 14 7 A 4	1803, 1807-1813 1819-1885
Kilcar	42	32	·0331, ·2278	5 C 1	188-222
Killaghtee	45	32	·0332, ·2279-80 ·2287, [·0807]	2 D 9 5 D 9	223-245
Killea	33	31	·0370 [·0836]	11 B 2	1389-1393
Killybegs Lower	41	32	·0333, ·0337 ·2281, ·2285, ·2292/3 [·0808/09]	6 C 4 5 D 12	246-261, 351 373-377
Killybegs Upper	44	32	·0334, ·2282, ·2286-7, [·0810]	5 E 9	262-284
Killygarvan	13	29	·0359, ·2323 [·0824]	12 G 13	562, 906-930, 786
Killymard	47	32	·0335, ·2283, ·2288 [·0811]	2 E 12	278, 285-315, 714
Kilmacrenan	15	29	·0360, ·2324 [·0825]	4 A 9, 9 C 7 12 F 3	802, 931-993
Kilteevoge Laghy (Drumhome)	37	31	·0371 [·2670]	15 C 2	1384-6, 1622-1644
Leck Letterkenny (Conwal)	30	31	·0372 [·3811]	9 G 6	863, 1394-1409
Lettermacaward	27	30	·0338, ·2294/95, ·2303	6 C 7	378-397
Malin (Clonca)			[·3812]		

PARISH	TITHES 1823–38 TAB 7/	FILM	VALUATION FIELD BOOKS 1830s OL4· HOUSE BOOKS [OL5·]	TENEMENT VALUATION c.1857 FICHE	1841–1851 CENSUS SEARCHES CEN S/7
Mevagh	11	28	·0361, ·2325	11 C 14	517, 994-1075
Mintiaghs (Barr of Inch)	19	29	·0351	8 G 10	650-653
Moville Lower	5	27	·0344 [·0814]	8 A 14	540-550
Moville Upper	6	27	·0345 [·0815]	8 C 11	551-562
Muff	13	30	·0352, ·2315	10 E 8	654-670
Raphoe	34	31	·0373, ·2333-5 [·0837/8]	10 B 3 13 G 6	1410-1445 1532, 1547
Raymoghy	34	31	·0374 [·0839/40]	10 A 3 11 B 6	1357-1667 1446-1486
Raymunterdoney	9	28	·0362, ·2326 [·0826]	14 A 13 4 A 11	1076-1094
Stranorlar	38	31	·0375, ·2336	15 D 8	1645-1660
Taughboyne	32	31	·0376 [·0841]	11 B 9 14 B 3	506, 1487-1527 1373, 1470
Templecarn	50	32	·0383	3 D 4	1886-1929
Templecrone	26	30	·0339, ·2304 ·2296/9	6 D 4	398-486
Templemore	20	29	·0364 [·0827/9]		
Tullaghobegley	8	28	·0363, ·2327 [·0830/1]	4 B 8	433, 1095-1319
Tullyfern	12	29	·0364, ·2328 [·0830/31]	12 B 11	768, 794, 1320-1344
Urney	40	32	·0377, ·2337	13 F 10	1661-1667

PARISH	TITHES 1823–38 TAB 23/	FILM	VALUATION FIELD BOOKS 1830s OL4· HOUSE BOOKS [OL5·]	TENEMENT VALUATION c.1858–61 FICHE	1841–1851 CENSUS SEARCHES SEARCHES CEN S/23/
Aghabog	12	82	1481/2 2967/8	4 D 10 5 E 12 8 G 12	241-291
Aghnamullen	18	82	1469/70 2963/4	2 C 8 3 E 2 5 D 6	1-87
Ballybay	17	82	1471/2 1502/3, [·3171]	4 A 4 3 A B	88-121
Castleblayney			[·3175]	2 G 11	
Clones	9	81	1483/4 1504/5 2969-76 [·1309/10] [·3172]	4 D 14 7 C 10 9 A 2	292-323 647-663
Clontibret	15	82	1473/4 2965 [·1308]	3 B 6 8 E 12	122-213
Currin	13	82	1485/6 2977-8	4 G 9 5 F 12	324-345
Donagh	2	81	1518 3012 [·1313]	6 C 8	797-812
Donaghmoyne	20	83	1492/3 2990	1 A 14 3 G 6	411-520
Drummully	11	82	1487	5 A 6	346-348
Drumsnat	5	81	1506-7 3003	7 D 8	664-666
Ematris	14	82	1488-9 2981	5 G 8	349-367
Emyvale			[·3177]		
Errigal Trough	1	81	1519 4437	4 B 8 6 F 5	813-866
Glaslough			[·3176]		
Inishkeen	21	83	1494 3002	9 B 13	521-542
Killanny	23	83	1496/7 2993/4	1 D 14	543-554
Killeevan	10	82	1490/1 2982/5	5 A 13 9 A 4	368-410
Kilmore	6	81	1508/9 3004	7 E 8	667-677

PARISH	TITHES 1823–38 TAB 23/	FILM	VALUATION FIELD BOOKS 1830s OL4· HOUSE BOOKS [OL5·]	TENEMENT VALUATION c.1858–61 FICHE	1841–1851 CENSUS SEARCHES CEN S/23/
Magheracloone	22	83	1498/9 2994/6	2 A 8	555-569
Magheross	19	83	1500/1 3001/2 [·3173/4]	1 E 11	570-646
Monaghan	7	81	1510/11 3005/6 [·1311] [·3178/80]	8 B 3	678-717
Newbliss			[·3181]		
Smithborough			[·3182/3]		
Muckno	16	82	1475/6 [·3175]	2 E 2	214-238
Tedavnet	3	81	1512/3 3010	6 G 10	718-765
Tehallan	4	81	1514/5 3011 [·1312]	8 A 2 8 G 7	239-240 766-770
Tullycorbet	8	81	1516/7	7 F 14 8 G 3	771-796

INDEX